# Psychology
# East and West

Edited by Swami Ajaya

Published by

THE HIMALAYAN INTERNATIONAL INSTITUTE
OF YOGA SCIENCE AND PHILOSOPHY
Honesdale, Pennsylvania

Library of Congress Catalog Card Number: 77-150850
ISBN 0-89389-019-7

Copyright 1976
First Printing, 1976
Second Printing, 1978

Himalayan International Institute
of Yoga Science and Philosophy
Honesdale, Pennsylvania 18431

# Contents

# Introduction

Each of our approaches to psychotherapy in the West focuses on a limited aspect of our total being and asserts its importance over other aspects of our functioning. One school emphasizes the uncovering of unconscious motivations, another directs itself toward changing behavior and a third stresses interpersonal relations. One approach asserts that insight into the source of one's present conflicts is a prerequisite for change, while another focuses on what the patient is experiencing in the present moment. Therapists of one persuasion believe in confronting the patient, while those of another advocate total acceptance. Some therapists encourage the intensification of emotions while others label emotional release "acting out" and prefer fostering sublimation. Certain schools of psychotherapy emphasize work with the physical body while others pay little attention to the body. A prospective patient is likely to be thoroughly confused in choosing between such diverse approaches as psychoanalytic, Rogerian, bioenergetic, trans-actional, behavioral, gestalt, Jungian, rational-emotive and numerous other schools of psycho-therapy. Each method seems to compete with the others in asserting itself as the most efficient process of inducing psychological growth; yet there seems to be no objective evaluation which compares and assesses these divergent schools of thought. Furthermore, there is almost no discussion of where these approaches are com-plementary or antithetical to one another.

In modern psychology we do not seem to have a comprehensive theory and methodology which considers all of the facets of human functioning and explains their proper place in the total per-son. But in the ancient psychology of yoga, such a comprehensive approach exists. Modern psychology seems to divide the person into different parts, each to be worked with by a different school. Thus each approach is partial and incomplete. But in yoga, teachers have for ages tried to understand and treat the whole person. Neither behavior, the unconscious, inter-personal relations, or one's emotional life is taken as the sole or primary target of intervention in leading the student toward growth. All are seen as important and are systematically dealt with.

Yoga is surely a system of psychotherapy, for

its whole aim and purpose is to lead man from unhappiness and suffering to a state of equanimity, in which he experiences lasting peace and joy. In this pursuit yoga psychology has put forth many of the theories and methods now being rediscovered by modern psychology. Conceptualizations of unconscious processes, theories of identification and role playing appear in the ancient textbooks, as do methods of bringing the unconscious into awareness, restructuring habits and overcoming anxiety. To a novice in the study of eastern psychology, the words, even their English translations, at first appear strange. Instead of reading about anxiety and tension we may encounter a discription of suffering and its causes; instead of memories we hear of *samskaras* or mental impressions. But a careful examination of the works of yoga psychology reveal that most of our current concepts were there long ago, though in slightly different forms. And these differences are of considerable value, for they open up new possibilities of reforming our way of understanding man. They make us aware of the hidden assumptions and limited conceptualizations in our own theories.

In contrast to modern psychology, yoga psychology has integrated the various aspects of human functioning into a comprehensive theory and therapeutic method. This includes techniques for working with the unconscious mind, habits, emotions, the physical body and interpersonal relations. Together these techniques become an integrated therapy to help the individual free himself from all those limitations which keep him from the realization of his full potential. For this reason it is not unusual for psychotherapists of such diverse persuasions as behavior therapy, psychoanalysis and gestalt therapy to find that their methods have much in common with yoga and that yoga extends their own theory into new and challenging areas. In addition, yoga psychology provides a perspective for bringing the various schools of psychotherapy together and for understanding how each contributes a part to the total comprehension of that complex creature called a human being.

In this volume psychotherapists with widely varied backgrounds who have considerable training and practical experience in yoga compare it with specific western approaches to psychotherapy. A psychiatrist with psychoanalytic training, a Jungian analyst, a counselor with expertise in behavior therapy and a psychologist experienced in leading encounter groups all find considerable similarity as well as some clear differences between yoga and their approach to psychotherapy.

In the first chapter the eight steps of Raja Yoga are used as a framework for comparing yoga with the techniques of psychoanalysis and later methods developed by Wilhelm Reich and Alexander Lowen. The author shows that psychoanalytic methods and yoga both deal with body posture, sensory withdrawal, the regulation of one's everyday life and the observation of mental processes. However, the methods developed to deal with these areas are in some ways strikingly different. In comparing these two methods of self-study, the author concludes that while in many respects their goals are in common, psychoanalysis stops far short of yogic training.

The second chapter takes a broader perspective and traces the development of psychoanalysis into the divergent schools developed by Adler, Jung, Horney and others. These approaches are compared with yoga in three areas: the method of free association, the underlying concepts of the nature of man, and the relationship between therapist and patient, master and disciple. The author, himself a Jungian analyst, points out that as our knowledge of psychological growth becomes more comprehensive, our theories and methods are evolving toward those of yoga.

This selection is followed by a chapter which

shows that the methods of behavior therapy are also similar to methods used in yoga. We are shown that both yoga and behavioral psychology learned a great deal from the study of animals, that both concern themselves with habits, and both have developed similar techniques for reducing anxiety. Yoga psychology, however, extended its theory to include mental habits as well as behavioral habits, an area which modern behavioral psychology is just beginning to consider. In this chapter the process of meditation is compared with the techniques of behavior therapy, and is found to be quite similar in many respects.

The final chapter is written by a psychologist who has considerable experience in leading groups which combine yoga and encounter techniques. Of particular interest is his comparison of the way in which an integration of yoga and encounter leads to a new way of understanding and dealing with emotions in the growth process. One of the most significant and unresolved questions in psychotherapy today revolves around how emotions should be handled. Should they be encouraged and even expanded, suppressed, or sublimated. Various therapies take quite different positions. The author of this chapter gives us still another alternative to dealing with emotions, one that has merit in helping to resolve this uncertainty.

Taken together, these four chapters give us an initial understanding of the scope of yoga as a comprehensive psychotherapy. They encourage us to seriously consider yoga as a systematic approach to understanding man's nature and how to treat him—an approach that can open new avenues for the growth and integration of psychology in the West.

Swami Ajaya
April 1, 1976

# Yoga and Psychoanalysis

*by*

Rudolph M. Ballentine Jr., M.D.

Psychology is man's effort to study his mind or psyche. Historically, it is a specialized branch of philosophy. Part of the task of the philosopher was to try and understand the mind. Only a small part of the mental activity that is studied in psychology occurs within an individual's conscious awareness. The rest of the mind is not known to the individual; it operates outside his field of awareness, so we call it "the unconscious mind." Of the various schools of psychology that have grown up in the West, only a few have recognized the existence of something called "the unconscious mind." There are many schools of psychology which deny that there is any such thing. They study the mind by looking at only the conscious part. They are interested in studying that which can be more easily observed and measured.

The unconscious mind has been most thoroughly studied in the West by the Psychoanalysts. Their interest in the unconscious is shared by the school of "Analytical Psychology", this being Jung's phrase for describing his offshoot from Freud's "psychoanalysis." In this country, however, it is primarily psychoanalysts who work with the unconscious mind, since analytical psychologists are numerically fewer and most practicing analysts are Freudian. Among the psychoanalysts, there has been a consistent effort over the last half century to deepen our understanding of the unconscious. The work continues systematically, and writers on the subject have amassed a growing body of literature and evolved a complex system of theory. Contrary to popular belief, psychoanalysis is not disappearing; the number of trained analysts has continued to grow at a slow but steady rate. Moreover, psychoanalysts continue to hold many of the more important teaching posts in academic and medical circles since their understanding of unconscious processes is unparalleled in the West.

In the East there are also many schools of psychology. Of those dealt with in Yoga, the ones that stem from Patanjali and from Vedanta (especially the writings of Shankaracharya), are of primary importance. They also acknowledge the existence of an unconscious mind, although they may use different words for it. In any case, there is an attempt in these traditions to come to terms with, to understand, to become aware of, the unconscious mind—not to limit the study of the mind to that of which one is ordinarily aware. There is then a similarity or parallel position between what might be called "Yoga psychology" in the East and what is called "Psychoanalysis" in the West. They hold analagous positions in the two cultures, each having been interested for some time in the task of studying the unconscious and how it moves men and sways nations. There is, however, a dramatic difference, for while psychoanalysis claims a tradition of perhaps a hundred years, Yoga psychology has a history of at least several thousand years. One might wonder about further differences: How would Psychoanalysis, which grew out of a *materially* oriented Western culture, reflect this perspective? What relevance and impact could the psychology of a less materialistic eastern culture have for Psychoanalytic theory? What are the possibilities for a synthesis?

If we look at these two traditions, we find that in terms of technique, there are some intriguing similarities. The system called Yoga by Patanjali is a series of eight steps: *Yama* and *Niyama* are often treated together because these are simply guidelines for behaving in the world in such a way as to facilitate the process of self-study and evolution; they help to manage existence in the world so it doesn't interfere with growth. Then there is something called *Asana*, with which most people who are aware of Yoga have some familiarity. *Asanas* are postures or "Yoga positions." Next comes the stage called *Pranayama*, which has to do with regulation of the breath and control of the energy one has at his disposal. This is followed by *Pratyahara*, which means the limitation of incoming stimuli, so as to decrease the attention given to the outside world and increase one's ability to focus on the inner world. Finally, there are three steps which can be termed *Concentration, Contemplation,* (the use of these terms varies) and *Meditation*. Although some people call all three "Meditation," actually these are three different degrees of focusing within. The final step, which is also called *Samadhi*, means focusing inward sufficiently to enter one of the higher states of consciousness, of which there are a number. Each of these eight stages brings up some interesting similarities or contrasts with regard to psychoanalysis.

Currently, much of psychotherapy is done sitting face to face with the therapist. But originally (and still today), the psychoanalyst who is working with the mind in more depth, meeting with a patient four times a week for many months or years, will almost always use a couch. The patient is asked to lie down and relax; he may have his eyes open, but he is in a reclining position, with the head a little bit elevated. This is done to facilitate free association so that the patient can become more aware of the thoughts passing through his mind and can then verbalize them. Originally, Freud, who developed psychoanalysis, used hypnosis; this was his method of getting a person to recall repressed and otherwise inaccessible aspects of himself. But he used it less and less as he found that people didn't recall afterwards what had happened during the hypnosis. He was striving for a more lasting awareness. So, he substituted a relaxed position for hypnosis. Asking the patient to lie down and let himself relax, he encouraged a "free floating" attention, an attitude of "just waiting to see" what would come into the mind.

In Hindi, the word *asan* means "easy"—an easy posture is an *asana*; it means a position that is comfortable and relaxed, easy to maintain, not

strenuous, and not stressful. After attempting
asanas, or yoga postures, one may have difficulty
believing that the word could possibly mean
"easy" since some of them are difficult at first.
Yet the whole purpose of the asanas is to help the
body become flexible enough to assume an easy,
comfortable position without tension. Actually,
any of the asanas, when properly done, is easy
and comfortable. If one is straining, he has not
yet perfected the posture he is attempting. In
Yoga, after the "cultural" or "loosening up
asanas" are mastered, then the meditative or
seated asanas are taught. By this time the student
should be able to assume the posture comfortably.
It is actually this relaxed, balanced, steady, seated
posture to which Patanjali refers when he used
the word *Asana* to indicate his third stage of Yoga
training.

It becomes apparent that these two techniques,
the couch and the *asana* are parallel. The point
in each case is to find some position that the
aspirant can assume so that his body tension
won't distract him, so that he can forget his body
and concentrate on what's going on at another
level. The purpose is to decrease body awareness.
The couch does that, and so does the *asana.*

In Yoga training, people who have trouble
sitting on the floor are sometimes encouraged

to use a reclining position, with the head elevated. This allows relaxation without encouraging sleep the way lying flat on the back does. All the old psychoanalysts, and even most of those practicing today, are careful to use couches (some of them have the couches built specially) so that the head is elevated at the proper angle and so the person remains relaxed yet alert.

The next stage of Yoga discipline includes practices and techniques for eliminating distracting sensory stimuli that come in from the external world—*Pratyahara*. This is also an important aspect of psychoanalytic treatment situations, where work is done with the unconscious. We must remove the more obvious sensory input to which the mind would respond if we are to see the subtler effects of the unconscious reveal themselves. There is an effort to eliminate all the distractions; and most psychotherapists will try to find an office, or situation, where they can work with a patient in quietness. One of the first things that the psychotherapist worries about is sound-proofing his office. He doesn't want the patient to be worried about who may be outside listening, and he doesn't want the patient to be distracted by noise from outside; he wants the patient to be able to just focus on himself and study himself without concern about the

outside world. This is the essence of *Pratyahara.*
*Pratyahara* is accomplished in the Yogic discipline,
primarily through a conscious control of sensory
input—simply cutting off awareness, ignoring it.
But one is always told when he begins to do
meditation: find a quiet place. Of course the
Yoga student does not have to be worried about
being overheard, since all his work is done in
silence. But he must manage nevertheless to
avoid having his attention occupied with the
sights and sounds of his surroundings. Patanjali
talks about voluntarily cutting off the inflow
of sensory stimulation, but one is not ready to do
that when he first begins, so he must find a place
that will decrease the distractions to such a
level that he's not fighting with them all the time;
otherwise, he will never have an opportunity to
develop the ability to cut them off voluntarily.

The work of John Lilly offers another interesting parallel here. He is a psychoanalyst, and his
attempts to deal with, to amplify or increase
access to the unconscious led him into the field
of sensory deprivation. For this work he used a
water tank.     Other researchers have used
chambers where subjects would sit in a dark,
sound-proof place, but Lilly used a tank in which
one could float in water. The basic principle is
to cut off input as much as possible. Similarly

in an isolation chamber, one wears guards over the hands so he doesn't feel anything, and the chamber is arranged so that there is no sense of touch, sound, or sight. In such a situation most people soon begin to hallucinate; it's a very common thing. Much of the research in this area was done by the Air Force because of an interest in what would happen when men were sent up in space. With both the tank and the isolation chamber, the results were the same: the conscious mind would sort of fall out of the picture. Since the person would cease to be processing information from the world, the conscious or "objective" mind would quiet down. Then memories, pictures, voices would begin to emerge from the unconscious. They would actually flood the conscious mind. The result would be experienced as dreams and memories, or it would be experienced as hallucinations, depending on the person's makeup. For some people, it was terrifying; for other people, it was fascinating. That depended on the structure of their psyches.

Some people realized: "Something is coming into my memory." Other people wondered "Where am I? I've been put into some other place; where have they taken me?" The isolation *forced* a sort of *Pratyahara*. Some people were ready for it and could benefit from the access to unconscious material. Others were not prepared, and were terrified and frightened. The danger of forcing into awareness unconscious material that cannot be constructively used is largely avoided in the Yogic training, since one learns to regulate the "isolation" voluntarily, by not *attending* to stimuli. The degree of isolation is then under control, and can be regulated according to his needs and level of maturity.

Now it might be instructive to drop back to the first steps of Yoga training, the *Yama* and *Niyama*. Yama means *control*, and these are guidelines for the beginner so that he can control his patterns of living in a way that will minimize turmoil, conflict and confusion and prevent further accumulation of the internal, unconscious "noise" with which he will have to cope. But the notion of telling a person how to live his life sounds repugnant to most therapists. They would say that a good therapist never tries to run your life. The more psycho-analytic and neutral one's stance, the less the therapists would be expected to interfere with the patient's life. The psycho-analyst is supposed to be the paragon of objectivity: "I'm just a neutral screen; I don't get involved; I just help you listen and observe . . ." But that's not literally true. In psychoanalysis, there is something called the "Rule of Absence."

For instance, if one is in the midst of analysis and suddenly decides to get married, his analyst will say, "No." And analysand will say, "What! What do you mean? Surely you're not telling me who to marry!" But the analyst will explain that there may be things going on in the analysis that have led the patient to seek out this relationship: "Why not wait a little while; don't get involved in something when you don't really know your motivations." People who are undergoing analysis are often counseled: "Don't make any major life changes during this time."

Another thing that an analyst will do is request patients to stop behavior that interferes with their work in the session. If a patient, for example, regularly seeks out a partner for sexual contact just before the therapy session, so that he comes in each time rather depleted and indifferent, the analyst cannot continue to say, "Well, let's just look at that." Finally, he will say, "It seems as though you're doing something that undercuts our ability to work. Something is going on there that uses all your energy. So maybe you should stop that, and then let's see what comes out in the session."

There has to be, even in psychoanalysis (and there is) a very systematic and deliberate insistence that the patient bring his conflicts and

problems into the therapy, rather than acting
them out in the world. And this is probably one
of the major things that guides any psychotherapist in dealing with a person's behavior
outside the session: he must make sure the
patient is not doing so much which is sick "out
there" that there is never a chance to look at it
"in here." And if he can prevent the person from
being "nutty" outside the session, if he can say,
"Be patient. You may feel like doing that, but
don't; don't do it and let's see what happens;
let's see if we can find out what's behind this,"
then before very long, some version of the same
problem will crop up inside the session in the
therapist-patient relationship. The patient is
acting more sensibly outside the session, but
suddenly he finds himself thinking: "Why are
you trying to do this to me?" Or, "I think you
charged me twice." Or something similar.
Suddenly, all his difficulties, his faulty ways of
relating, begin to emerge between himself and the
therapist, which is exactly what the therapist
wants; this must happen, otherwise there will
never be a chance to look at them, except indirectly and theoretically. Now the problem is in
the room, in the therapeutic session, and we can
say, "Huh, what is this? I wonder what's happening; let's see if we can figure it out." Otherwise,

it's "out there" and it can never be dealt with properly.

The practices Yama and Niyama are parallel to those controls that the therapist must require. There is a definite similarity between the approaches. In both cases, there is an attempt to regulate life outside so that the self-study can be more productive. It doesn't matter whether the self study takes place in meditation or whether it is done in the psychotherapeutic stiuation; it is still necessary to frustrate one's neurotic tendencies in the world in order to productively resolve them—whether during work with a therapist or work in meditation. It's a difficult point; not difficult because it's intellectually hard to understand, but difficult because nobody wants to understand it. It has a rather drastic effect on one's life if he ever really understands it.

If the analyst's "Rule of Abstinence" and prohibition of "acting out" have their counterparts in the first steps of Yoga training, the Yamas and Niyamas go a step further. They not only provide for curtailment of activities that would interfere with the work of self analysis, they also help eliminate the creation of new conflicts, new emotionally-laden memories that will require more work and resolution. They are hints on regulating one's patterns of interacting and one's behavior so that the mass of repressed unconscious material is no longer being constantly increased.

The cautions against violence, lying, etc., which are part of the Yamas and Niyamas, are not based on moralistic grounds, but are in the very practical interest of maintaining an input into the unconscious that will be neither burdensome, threatening nor difficult to confront at a later time. It amounts to a sort of "stacking the deck" so that the cards that are to be flipped up from the unconscious will be good ones! This is an educational and preventative aspect of Yoga that goes beyond what the analyst feels himself qualified to offer or justified in suggesting.

The next phase of training in Yoga is called *Pranayama*. The word *Pranayama* means literally "control of *prana*." It is usually thought of as a process of working with the breath. We've seen parallels above between the initial steps of yoga training and certain aspects of psychoanalysis and we will see similar parallels to the last three steps, Concentration, Contemplation, and Meditation, since they deal with turning the attention inward to look at the mind. But pranayama is different, with the possible exception of some of the breathing techniques that are taught in behavior therapy or bioenergetics, there's nothing like pranayama in Western psychotherapy. Certainly there is no analyst who spends time working with breathing. The bioenergetic therapists do talk some about breathing, and work with it to some extent. Of course, the founder of that school, Alexander Lowen, was a psychoanalyst by training, but he doesn't consider himself an analyst anymore.

Actually, Lowen's emphasis on the "bioenergy" that is affected by breathing patterns and posture moves his work closer to that of Yoga. For pranayama is far more than breathing exercise. Pranayama is, in fact, something quite different. Unfortunately, it's very difficult to teach Pranayama. But it is, by contrast, very easy to teach breathing exercises. So we ordinarily teach breathing exercises with the hope that people will work with them enough to discover what Pranayama is. Pranayama is often associated with breathing, but it need not be. It's possible to stop breathing and still do Pranayama. But breathing is the best entry into the area of Pranayama.

In the West we deal with the Mind in our study of psychology; this is something that is fairly developed here, after a fashion. And we certainly have studied the body, very elaborately. We have scrutinized it and named all the little pieces and particles; we can't be accused of neglecting it. But somewhere between these two levels of our being, there is another level of functioning. According to Eastern thought, whether it's Chinese, Zen, Indian, Tibetan, whatever, there is this other level of our existence which is called Energy, or *Prana*. This is neither physical, nor is it mental. Although there is a Mind and there is a Body, there is a relationship between them. And this relationship comes through the intermediate stratum of being that is called in Yoga theory, *Prana.*

There are techniques for controlling the physical, e.g., asanas, various exercises, etc. Many of these have Western parallels. There are also techniques for working with the mind in meditation: techniques for disciplining it, controlling it, learning concentration, and learning how to dig into the unconscious. These also have their counterparts in modern psychotherapy. But in addition, there are in Yoga, techniques for dealing with the level of energy, controlling and regulating it, altering it. These techniques are called "the control of prana" (Yama means control). Pranayama is the direct alteration, control, regulation, modulation of this set of energy phenomena. This has no parallel in psychoanalysis. It's almost surprising that it doesn't, since Freud's original notion of psychic energy or *libido*, freeing it from a strictly sexual meaning, suggesting that it could be used for less instinctual and more creative pruposes (sublimation), he was approaching even more closely the idea of *prana*. It's puzzling that he didn't stumble upon the relationship between breathing patterns and the way in which energy or *libido* was used and experienced.

It was only through the work of Wilhelm Reich and his student Lowen that the study of this energy came back into focus—and some rough techniques were developed to regulate and direct it. If Lowen's writings are studied chronologically, it will be found that his thinking is gradually approaching the ancient Yogic descriptions of prana and chakras. Despite this, however, his techniques using the breath to affect energy flow are crude by comparison with the detailed and complex writings found on the subject in the ancient Samskrit texts.

We should consider the parallel between the Psychoanalyst and the levels of training in Yoga which involve working directly with the Mind, learning to focus the concentration, learning to go deeply into uninterrupted concentration and then learning to follow back up, into higher levels of consciousness so as to transcend the

Mind itself. Of course, psychoanalysis involves a delving into the inner world. And, of course, it demands concentration and the development of an astute and honest capacity for self-examination. Yet psychoanalysis stops far short of the ambitions of Yogic training. Psychoanalysis aims only for a modest (though significant) reorganization of the unconscious, removing some of the obstacles to satisfactory functioning in the world. It makes no claims to carry one to "higher states of consciousness." Yoga does. What accounts for this vast difference in their goals?

Basically, the problem is this: that the Mind is a World of Words. The major aspect of what we call Mind is words and symbols. That's what it's made of and what it's use is. Its whole universe is words. Psychoanalysis is based on the exchange of words. I lie down and I say words, and the analyst listens. And every now and then, he says a word or two, or sometimes more. Then he falls silent and I say some more words. Words, words, and more words . . . And this we call "working with the Mind": get in there where the words are and toss them about. But there's a different system of dealing with the Mind in Eastern traditions, and this system is not based on use of words but is based on observing the Mind from a point *above* the mind. This means entering a state of consciousness where no words are used; no words are thought; no words mediate the awareness; awareness is *without* the medium of words; awareness is non-verbal. The sages of the East, people who have worked in this area, people who have devoted their lives to using this method, have found that, by looking from this perspective, more can be learned in a shorter time with much more clarity than if one is still down there all mixed in with the words. The traditional simile compares someone who is in a valley mixed in with the people, vegetation and the physical features of the terrain with someone who is up on a hilltop looking down. The lay of the land and the location of each person in it is much more easily grasped from above. The problem with psychoanalysis and psychotherapy is that they are limited by the use of words, and using words to deal with words and deal with thoughts becomes often frustratingly circular. Such are the limitations of the method. In both Yoga and psychoanalysis attention is turned within and the attempt in both cases is to study the inner world; but soon thereafter the similarity ends because the techniques are different, and they end up accomplishing quite different things.

One last aspect in the comparison between

Yoga and psychoanalysis is the relationship
between the therapist and the patient and how
it compares with the relationship between the
guru and his student. There are books on self-
analysis and some people say Yoga can be mastered without a teacher, that it can be learned from
a book. But there's something that happens in
the relationship between the teacher or therapist
and the student or patient that is necessary.
There must be some field for playing out ones
problems; otherwise the whole pursuit tends to
become intellectual. It can become intellectual
even with the therapist, and this happens often,
in which case one thinks he's been analyzed or
therapized, and can talk a lot at cocktail parties,
but really has no insight. So he continues acting
the same way and feeling the same way. Although
on the surface things may have shifted about a
little so as to give the illusion of change, basically
the game remains the same. But there is something
that goes on between two people that is usually
necessary for genuine progress to occur. Another
person (who has the wisdom necessary for the
work) can pull one loose from his repetitive ways.
  Change has to come from outside, thus the
need for the guru or for the therapist. But
"outside" here simply means "outside" one's
present psychological organization. Otherwise

one continues doing the same thing; though he may change the way he does it, he has not himself changed. True change comes from moving to some point within oneself that is outside of what he was aware of before. In Yoga, we talk about the guru as a person and then we talk about the guru within; and the true guru is not the person in the world. Rather, the true guru is a level of consciousness within ourselves; it's beyond what we are using at this point.

In actuality, the same point is made by psychoanalysts. The therapist observes and studies the patient's mind. The patient's therapy is *primarily* a process of incorporating and internalizing the observer (the observing ego). Perhaps more accurately we might say that it's a process of discovering within oneself the capacity for such observation. The primary difference between meditation and psychoanalysis is the level to which this observation is led. And it is here, perhaps, where an investigation of the process of meditation might be most productive for the psychoanalyst.

# The Development of Psychotherapy

*by*

Arwind U. Vasavada, Ph.D.

The trends in the different schools of psycho-therapy are moving in the direction of Eastern wisdom and opening a way for better and closer understanding between the East and West. It will be clear from the brief account I shall give, that a sincere scientific attitude, honestly pursued, leads to fundamental truths of life. And it should open the eyes of many of us in whose life the synthesis between science and traditional spiritual lore has not yet occurred.

The progress of different schools of psycho-therapy in modern times in the West is bringing into greater clarity the fact that the causes of psychiatric illness are to be found in the aliena-tion of man from himself. Beginning with Freud, going characteristically the scientific objective way, the West has gradually laid, step by step, the foundation for a system and a method which has brought it unconsciously nearer to the spiritual root of Eastern wisdom, the knowledge of Self. We can confidently say that the psychotherapies of the future will become one of the strongest bridges between East and West.

The rapidly changing geography of the world with its consequent changes in interpersonal relations takes man unawares in his habitual mode of behavior and demands greater resilience in his attitude towards himself and the world, which is not always easy to bring forth voluntarily. It, therefore, produces undue strain upon him. Such a constant demand does not leave much time to recollect, to take stock of things and carry his whole being in an integrated form to meet the need of the changing environment within and without. As a result man begins to live on his surface rather than from his depths. His life becomes flat and two dimensional. Such a situation produces a gradual split within him, between his depth and the surface, and lays the foundation for later mental disorders of minor or major kinds.

Man tends to forget what he essentially is and begins to believe himself to be a system of inter-actions with the environment. He thinks he is adjusting and adjusted to the world, but in fact, he is living by defenses. He is living a life of falsity, because it is merely reactive. Unless he comes to realize this and turns inward to recognize his depth and disidentify himself from the false wrappings of his adaptations, he cannot start building his natural personality and be the man he is. The neurotic or psychotic has begun to live in his fantasies at the cost of the realities of life. He sees the world from a wrong standpoint because he has learned to look upon himself wrongly. Unless he is prepared to discover himself, he cannot get free from the disorder. Almost all the systems of psychotherapy, beginning with Sigmund Freud, have striven as their initial step to deeper analysis to make man aware of his defenses and discover his natural heritage. It becomes the task of the therapist to slash one by one the false wrappings with which he has covered himself. This is exactly parallel to the procedure a *guru* adopts with the seeker. The *guru's* first task is to cut asunder the bonds and the veils in which the seeker has shrouded himself and to let him gaze at his own naked self.

## Psychoanalysis

Freudian psychoanalysis aims to make the analysand conscious of the defenses he has been building since childhood against the Oedipus situation. His early emotional relations with parents and siblings have colored the world view which he carries with himself as a means of adapting to the changing demands of the world. It leads him more and more into complications and away from the realities of the world. He thus begins to live in the world of his own imagination and fancy with a complete or partial break with reality. The process of analysis brings self-awareness and the recognition of what he really is and the reality of life and teaches him to adapt his erotic drives in conformity with his environment.

With Freud, self-discovery, thus, becomes essential to correct living. One may not agree with him in the understanding of man as a bundle of libidinous strivings of an erotic nature, but one has to acknowledge Frued's belief in the need for self-discovery as a means of correct living.

Not only that, it is to the credit of Freud that he discovered a correct method—the method of free association—a tool for everyone who wished to understand himself. All other previous methods of abreaction and hypnosis kept the man dependent upon the doctor, whereas the method of free association was a sort of torch in the hands of men to enable them to enter the hinterland of the mind. Though born and bred in the

extroverted, scientifically oriented culture of the
West, he initiated the way for introversion and
meditation, a distinctly oriental approach towards
the psyche. I think it was the first and most
important step in the history of psychotherapy
in the West. It gradually opened the way to the
discovery of the depth and richness of the psyche.
The method of free association released man from
the compulsion of external and internal demands
of life and mind. It gave him the opportunity
to look within and discover the inner dynamics
of mind. It is, however, a different question
when one asks how far this method was used and
developed by Freud and by the Freudians.

Freudian psychoanalysis also brought into relief
another important aspect of therapy, the doctor-
patient relationship—the transference situation.
The patient involved the doctor in the maelstrom
of his conflict, which the doctor could rise
above, to the extent he himself was free from
those conflicts within. This situation led to the
need of the analyst being analysed before under-
taking treatment of any patient. Otherwise the
analyst fell into the danger of becoming disturbed
himself, or exaggerating the conflicts of the
patient and spoiling the case. Thus, with unusual
insight, Freud touched upon a problem of great
importance in the process of self-discovery.

However, it was left to others to discern the delicacy and intricacy of this problem. The relationship between himself and the goal is a relation between the two—a more or less dispassionate guide who educates the other into correct living and a disturbed person. Again, the education given is not merely intellectual. It is based on experiencing, something very much akin to that found between master and disciple.

To summarize, Freudian psychoanalysis evolved a method akin to oriental yoga, a method of interpretation to gain understanding of the defenses with which man has covered his libidinous drives. It is a method which reveals the structure of personality depths of which man has remained ignorant. Freud also showed us the importance of the transference situation. But the one-sided understanding of man espoused by Freud came to be recognized and criticised during his lifetime and one of his close associates evolved a different theory about man.

Adler, interested in organ inferiorities and observing the compensatory function in the living organism, applied it to the understanding of man. From childhood, according to Adler, a child is faced with an environment in which he felt inferior and powerless. The elders of the home ruled and were powerful and free. They could do what they liked. In every respect the child was unfree and unable to do anything he chose because he was handicapped by his relative lack of knowledge, strength and intelligence. Early interpretation of these situations paved the way for a style of life and later neurotic disorders. An exaggerated sense of inferiority moved him to compensate by setting up a goal of superiority—a fictitious goal to be achieved in life. Later he turns away from the realities of life and imagines himself superior to others in certain respects. He arranges his strivings in such a manner that he could never achieve the goal. Outwardly he seems to be sincerely striving for something superior, but unconsciously he ever tries to avoid it. He so arranges his life that he does not permit himself to be tested and the blame for non-accomplishment does not come to him but falls to the world. But for this little thing or that, he would have achieved his goal. "Poor me," he is blameless. Therapy with the Adlerians consists in piercing through these arrangements and self-deceptions and making the patient aware of them so that he may recognize himself as he is and look at the world realistically, starting afresh the task of adjustment in conformity with reality.

Despite differences in viewpoints of what man's nature is—Adler understanding man to be governed by a power motive as against the erotic drive in the case of Freud, Adlerian and Freudian therapy seek the same result—the recognition of man as he is. According to Freud, after the false vestures are cast aside, man is revealed to be in constant conflict between instinctual drives of the Id and social, moral and other cultural forces, which themselves are sublimated aspects of the libidinous drives. The Adlerian analysis reveals man to be charged with a drive for power which, if utilized in conformity with the world, makes man live a normal life.

## The Method of Free Association

In spite of all the criticism against Freud, he was the pioneer in this field. He initiated a method which revealed the hidden depths of the human mind, widened our scope of understanding of human nature and paved the way for further development in this field. The method of free association is characteristically eastern in nature. The patient reclining, relaxed in the analytical couch, giving free reign to his associations, is diverted from the rationally directed thinking which is characteristically western. He is asked to go inward and to soak into whatever is coming from within. The freely directed association

trains man in a way of attention which could
lead him gradually to the path of expanded
awareness.

In the early period with Freud this method was
employed to understand symptoms and dreams.
It became a valuable tool to pierce through the
defenses and to uncover the falsities of man. Jung
very correctly remarked that it is invaluable in
revealing the shadow side of man. In the Horney
school this method deepens and becomes a way
of being. It makes man aware of paradoxes and
becomes a way of communing—a unitary process
as opposed to dichotomous process. This aspect
of free association has deeper spiritual significance
in so far as it revolutionizes the whole attitude
and the way of thinking, the characteristic
western subject/object way of thinking which is
detrimental to self-realization. It is a process in
which the subject gradually loses itself into a
single unitary entity.

The analytical psychology of Jung neither
made use of this approach nor the couch of
classical psychoanalysis. He believed in the
face-to-face confrontation between the patient
and the analyst. He called for association by the
patient permitting ramification of thinking into
available memories. He extended the scope of
this method in his interpretations at the subjective

level.  Here the doctor helped the patient in associating the material by supplying from his own fund of knowledge.  The face-to-face confrontation with the patient brings the personality of the doctor into prominence.  The doctor is no more passive listener to free associations who hints at interpretations when necessary, but an active cooperator in the process of healing. This change in associating was called in due to the discovery of archetypes and the objective psyche—the unconscious of far deeper significance than what Freud had discovered.

Experiencing conflict honestly without any attempt to avoid it is recognized by Jungian psychotherapy.  In solving the problems of the later stages of analysis, Jung emphasized that it is by going through the sufferings of being involved in the dualities of life that the transcendent function can be activated and the experiencing of higher unities made possible.  In certain cases he advised active imagination so that the unconscious  archetypal material might be assimilated. Suffering meaningfully undertaken is a kind of *tapasya** which purifies man.  The value of suffering and *tapasya* is also recognized by the

---

* One of the practices followed in yoga, which is often translated as austerity.

Dasein school. They believe that there is no
escape from the misery of man's existential
situation. He must face it squarely and boldly.
Correct meaning of life comes from purified
vision. If we go deeper into this process we shall
find that guided imagination can release man
from his compulsions and conditioning.

## The Nature of Man

One of the important contributions of Freud
was his empirical demonstration of the unconscious and the use of this term in understanding
human nature. Man is more than a mere ego,
conscious only of its exterior strivings and behavior. He is determined to a great extent by a
part of his being, which he doesn't know about—
the unconscious. It was left to Jung to discover
the deeper layer of the unconscious and its im-
plications. But Freud paved the way. Freud
understood man to be ridden with libidinous
drives from which he could not escape. Man's
life can only be a compromise with these impulses
because only a part of its energy can be channeled
into higher forms. According to Adler, analysis
revealed man as a social being who can adjust
himself to environment and become a useful
member of society if he can avoid becoming

involved in compensatory drives to suppress imagined inferiorities. He does not explain why man is caught in this conflict. Adler says that normal man also lives by fictions, but they are workable and practical. A neurotic lives by fictions which are unattainable because they are totally unrealizable.

With Jung the picture of man changes. There is no self-deception practiced by the unconscious upon man. Here the unconscious is helpful, being more than a repository of repressed and forgotten material. The unconscious is the origin of consciousness and the rich soil from which man can draw all he needs to transform himself and reach selfhood. The basic opposition between the conscious and the unconscious which gives rise to all other dualities and opposites which involve man in suffering and misery is not absolute. The dualities in life are two sides of an identical thing, hence relative to the standpoint of man. Such an understanding of man gives a different orientation to the ills of man. In the malady itself are contained the seeds for regeneration of man and of his creative possibilities. Jung found in these opposites a natural dynamic process which he called the individuation process. This is a process which man can utilize if it is his destiny and become a whole man. For Jung

the unconscious becomes the source of spiritual
life and deep mystical, religious experiences.   It
is man's onesided emphasis on partial personality
systems within and without which involves him
in all sorts of conflicts and absurdities in life.
If man has the strength and capacity to go through
the    suffering    of    these    identifications    and
consequent meaninglessness of life and relativity,
the unconscious helps him to transcend all conflicts and lead him to the state beyond opposites.
As man frees himself from the bonds of the outer
realities of the collective conscious and the inner
realities of the collective unconscious, his horizon
widens and he gets an opportunity to experience
the Self.

Freud disillusioned western man from the mis-
understanding and self-satisfaction that he is the
ego and it is everything.  He showed a deeper side
to his personality, the dreaming, the unconscious
side.  From the state of waking life he brought
man to understand that he is also the dreamer of
his dreams at night and that this is an important
part of his personality.  Jung through his method
of active imagination showed a still deeper side
of the unconscious and confronted man with the
dreamless state.  The analytical process if pursued
carefully and sincerely led man to experience
what he called the "Night Sea Journey."  Jung

never wrote about the Fourth State—*Turiya*\*— in his books. He could not understand it till very late. One knows through personal communications that his last days were spent in unravelling the mystery of this state in which his study of Zen Buddhism played an important part.

Karen Horney looks at man from a different angle. Man is neither ridden with irreconcilable conflicts between pleasure and reality principles nor with the drive for power, but he is involved in strivings of an opposed nature which is of his own making. Still there is within him potentiality to realize his self. This can free him from neurotic conflicts. Because of the basic anxiety arising out of feeling helpless and isolated in a potentially hostile world, man develops neurotic trends of a contradictory nature. He turns towards submission, aggression or detachment compulsively to solve his basic anxiety. These contradictory trends lead him further into vicious circles of deeper conflicts between his imagined and the real self. Man is thus led into greater falsity and further away from realizing his self. Horney calls this the process of self-alienation. By understanding his false attitude and behavior one can

---

\*   In yoga terminology, this **fourth state** of transcendent consciousness, beyond waking, dreaming and dreamless sleep is called *turiya*.

arrive at Self-Realization. There is always hope and redemption for man according to Horney. Man must be prepared for honest self-examination and go through the sufferings of giving up his false gains and imagined realities. Developments in the Horney school make it quite clear that the therapeutic process tends to annul every kind of dichotomy and leads man to experience the total awareness of himself. In this technique a client is asked to focus his attention within himself in order to feel organically what is going wrong with him; he is asked to stop his chatterbox mind, which is creating all the surface whirlpool not allowing us to experience fully. Geldin asks the client to remain silent for some time and to give a complete shift in the direction of his attention. Man has cut himself off from his organic unity— his identity. The focusing starts the process of experiencing in the therapeutic situaion, and, as the fullness of experiencing gradually frees him, he becomes more detached, less involved, and is able to look at himself and his situation.

Man's behavior is conditioned by his *samskaras*, of past impressions in the mind. The technique of Yoga helps free man from this bondage. In one of the Yoga techniques, an initiate is asked to sit calmly and watch the flow of his mind. He is asked neither to take interest in and follow a pleasing thought or fantasy nor to avoid or negate a displeasing thought. He should allow his mind to flow in the direction it likes; he should try to become a spectator, an onlooker of the drama of his mind being unfolded. If the mind is thus allowed to flow, it will come to stop automatically when its dynamism is spent and not reinforced either by following it or avoiding it. This initial practice and other auxiliaries aim to decondition the mind completely so that one is able to discriminate between the psychological processes and the Self in its unconditioned state. Dr. Gendlin's technique is similar to the above and it is no wonder that it brings good results.

The psychotherapeutic process in the West has imposed limitations upon itself, which seem to be called forth by the nature of the problem the client brings, and by the limited goal which seems satisfying to the therapist in the present situation. Such a limitation does not provide for further exploration into the nature of human personality and those end results of the process of transformation which starts once some insight has been gained by the client. It is because of this limitation that the goal and aim of psychotherapies in the West seem to be different from that of any process of personality change in the East.

This limitation, however, does not hold true

for some psychologists like Jung, Harold Kelman, and R. Assagioli. Significant contribution has been made by Dr. Jung in this exploration. His patients continued to work upon themselves even after the analysis was over. This and Jung's continuing exploration of his own personality brought him to the deeper level of man's personality. Jung showed that the problems of the first half of life are different from those of the second half. If the problems of the first half consist of the founding of the family, in establishing a useful position in the society and the like, then the problem of the second half consists in finding the meaning of life and death. He very clearly brought to our notice that once the therapeutic process starts, and if the man is sincere and honest, it takes him naturally to seek his individuation. It is a natural process, none can escape it since the very movement of the psyche offers opportunity to move forward. Of course, it rests with us to take up this call or not. It also is very true that until we have reached our fullest realization we are restless and spiritually disquiet. He has shown how our limited outlook, our identification with the outer and the inner world, blocks this natural movement of the ongoing process. Dream interpretation, active imagination and like methods, with him, aim ultimately to help one disidentify himself from the objects of the outer and the inner realm, so that the ego is able to find its rightful place in the scheme of his psychic organization and discover the source of energy which moves the psyche.

Jungian ideas about the latter stage in life compare very well with Indian thought. Indian tradition holds out a fourfold ideal of life for man, known as *Dharma, Artha, Kama,* and *Moksa.* In the first half of life man is required to satisfy his natural propensities and be a useful citizen. By rightful means he has to earn his living to support himself and the family; this is fulfilling the ideal of *Artha.* He has also to satisfy his natural urges in a right way. By fulfilling this ideal of *Kama,* or desire, he has the opportunity not only to satisfy his desires but to associate himself with a larger whole than his family, since founding the family enlarges the scope of relationship and obligations. Each man is supposed to achieve these ideals of *Kama* and *Artha* in the first half of life. With the advent of the second half, when many of his obligations to the family are over and he has established his position in society, his scope of activities is still enlarged. He becomes aware of the larger whole—the universe. In order to fulfill this responsibility he has to be guided by *Dharma*

his duty towards the world. Indian thought
goes still deeper than this humanistic ideal in so
far as it holds liberation as the final and supreme
goal of life, which, without this fulfillment, is
incomplete. Thus the goal of liberation held out
by Indian thought and that of Individuation by
Jung show very clearly the similarity of thinking
in the two. The process of analysis once started
and if continued rightly, inevitably leads man to
his self-discovery and that is his natural goal.

A confused mind needs to get calm and tranquil, since it is only then that it can assess its
situation correctly. All the methods, from
free association to focusing and active imagination
train man to withdraw from the outgoing activity
so that he may get in touch with his inner calm
which is the source of all activities. He is, in
fact, trained to detach himself from his involve-
ments with his problems and situations, so that
he may return to his natural calm and tranquility,
and be aware of it. It is a voluntary process.

The return to natural calm occurs also in sleep,
through the effect of drugs and also at the end of
every activity. Whenever a man gets tired or
bothered by a problem, he goes to sleep and
wakes up refreshed and replenished. Sleep
overcomes him. Psychiatrists prescribe drugs to
bring the patient to similar tranquility. Here,

due to the effect of drugs, sleep also overcomes a man. But the man is not transformed either by sleep nor by the drug. He wakes up the same troubled man, with his problems unsolved.

The difference between the calm attained through sleep or drugs, and the one attained through yogic methods is that in the yogic process it is brought about with awareness and in the others, it occurs without awareness. The awareness of calm through yogic process has the advantage that the person begins to be aware of his true identity as that which transcends all the dualities of life. The yogic process brings us to the awareness of our natural calm which is also the awareness of ourselves. A man who remains in his natural calm and full awareness is alert and receptive. He becomes related to the world without confusion and preconceptions. With the gradual maturation this awareness becomes total and man finds himself in a state of Oneness and harmony with all.

## The Guide

We shall now take up the last part of our discussion, the doctor-patient relationship. With the advance of knowledge, Freud became conscious of the peculiar relation developing between

doctor and patient. He saw its immense importance in the therapeutic process. The remark
he made to Jung when both were on a lecture
tour in America in their early days of association
makes the point clear. He meant to say that if
one understood transference he understood
psychoanalysis. Confidence and emotional
rapport with the analyst is necessary for any
successful analysis. The delicacy of the transference situation necessitated that the analyst
be analysed before he undertook analysis. The
image of the doctor as it emerged in Freudian
psychotherapy is that of a dispassionate guide
who is more or less free from the conflicts he is
supposed to treat. According to Freud the
emotional situation in transference is centered
round the Oedipal situation. And thus it was
a sort of reactive behavior that developed
between the two, patient and doctor. The doctor-
patient relationship with Freud did not go
beyond the limited part of each one's personality.
The relation remained formal and distant in spite
of being intimate.

With Jung the transference situation took a
deeper meaning. Jungian psychotherapy extended
beyond the field of the so-called abnormal
patients. In solving the problems of the later
half of life of a normal man, it becomes a process

of turning man to reach his center—the Self. With this, a deeper spiritual meaning was discovered in this situation. It was not merely a situation in which one gave and the other received. It turned out to be an archetypal situation in which both were in the powerful grip of some numinous, transpersonal factor. This situation demanded as much self-examination on the part of the analyst as it did of the patient. It was an opportunity to further realization of the self, its depth and richness. Anything like cocksureness on the part of the analyst would be detrimental for both. Thus in Jungian psychotherapy the transference situation becomes a steady and constant opportunity for self-awareness. One must be alert lest he fall into fossilized static self-assurance. The same aspect of the transference situation and its importance is hinted at by Kelman when he says that if analysis does not change the doctor from what he was it is not an analysis. Continual self-knowledge and alertness are characteristic of a correct analytical procedure. We thus see that the dichotomy of doctor-patient and that of the basic dichotomy of subject/object gets slowly dissolved with Jung in the transference situation and makes for the fusion of the two personalities. It prepares for the experiencing of the non-dual, transcending the limited personalities of the two.

.Eastern wisdom also asserts that man cannot live well and usefully by practicing self-deception, by identifying himself with external as well as internal roles, one given to him by society and the other by his inner system of *samskaras**. The life of compulsion and drivenness can only bring misery and unhappiness. Every attempt to free oneself and gain his independence based on false attitudes towards others and compulsiveness to do something leads to greater involvement in the vicious circle. He has to become aware of his falsities, difficult and full of suffering as this may be. This is what a *guru* does to a disciple. It is a cutting of his bonds, uncovering of false veils of ignorance. This makes him aware of his distinction from the body. Deeper analysis of archetypal contents leads a step further to the awareness of one's distinction from the dreaming or imagining state or the subtle body. Further deeper analysis and understanding confronts man with his emptiness—*Sunyata*, the typical experiencing of the Night Sea Journey. Without guidance this could be experienced as in the Existential Neurosis, as a feeling of general mean-inglessness of life and suffering caused by the

---

* Unconscious tendencies.

sense of utter loneliness in the dark and dreary world.

Modern psychotherapies have also tried to understand these experiences in their healthy and neurotic aspects. It has become evident to all serious psychotherapists today that man is not what he appears to be or what he thinks himself to be. Behind the upper crust of ego, intellect and self-consciousness, there is a deeper man within, who is the life and origin of the upper structure. It is by turning to it that man can gain the necessary strength, knowledge and the wisdom to solve problems and live a decent civilized life. The key to the solution of human suffering is not outside but within him, he only needs to look within.

Though wisdom is within him, man needs to be directed by a guide who is dispassionate and already advanced in self-knowledge, and who does not sit in absolute judgment upon him. The guide is not merely a person but an image of something transpersonal. The one in whose wisdom and magic power of healing the student has such confidence and to whom he devotedly surrenders and feels bound by strong emotional ties of strange, unqualified nature is not the man before him, but the transpersonal archetype of Self or God, in terms of Jung and the *guru* in the yogic

way of thinking. If the student does not con-
cretize his *guru* and god in the person of the
external guide, he can discover the same within
himself, and from then on his guide is always
within him. Intimate disinterested personal
relationship between the *guru* and *sisya* have from
time immemorial been the steps to realize the
transpersonal within.

One of the fundamental requirements in
Rogerian therapy is that a therapist should be
able to give wholehearted, non-evaluative acceptance to the client. For a therapist a client is of
unconditioned worth. It is this situation which
permits the meaningful interaction. The process
of personality change begins to take place and the
client is able to unfold himself and accept himself
as he is. The therapist, by accepting him as of
unconditioned worth, without his personal likes
and dislikes, is able to awaken the client to his
own unconditioned worth. The client, in the
whirlpool of outgoing activity and the pursuit
of external aims, has lost his identity, has begun
to value things and situations more than his own
person. The therapist, by giving the required
unqualified acceptance enables the client to
recognize his worth, his lost identity, so that he
can live an authentic life.

In trying to understand this heavy demand

upon a therapist, I ask myself who can accept the other wholeheartedly? Who can be so above his personal likes and dislikes? The client may be very ugly and uncouth, may have displeasing manners. He may say something which touches upon the therapist's own weakness. Is it possible to accept the other unconditionally just by assuming a role, a pose for a short duration? Is it merely a question of taking on the role of a therapist and casting it away after the therapeutic session is over? We are sure to agree that this is not so.

I feel that that person alone can give his whole-hearted acceptance to the other who is generous enough to give undemanding love. He is the one for whom love means continual, joyful, and unbidden giving alone. He is so full of it that love gushes out of him like a fountain. We can thus see that one who is truly an embodiment of love, one who has risen above his likes and dis-likes alone can fulfill such a tremendously responsible task of a therapist. It becomes very clear that a psychotherapist has to live up to what he practises.

It must be evident from what has been said that in the role of the therapist we are approaching the role of master in the master-disciple situation. A master is supposed to be a living example of what he teaches. He has realized his true identity, oneness with the universe, and is overflowing with an abundance of love and compassion for all. He is a balanced person who does not react to a situation, but responds creatively to it. This is because he has transcended the opposites of personal preferences and is immersed in the very fountain of love. He does not treat the disciple as a disciple but as his own Self. He believes that the disciple has simply lost his identity. In truth, he is not different from *Brahman*, the Infinite. The Master is thus able to accept the other with an even mind.

## Conclusion

We have tried to trace the progress of the psychotherapies of Freud, Adler, Jung, Horney and others taking into account three points for discussion, the therapeutic method, the understanding of man and the doctor-patient relationship. From this brief review it should be evident to us that psychotherapies in the West have moved and progressed consciously and unconsciously towards those very methods and understanding of man which are close to the spiritual tradition of self knowledge in the East. It seems that psychotherapies, if taken to their

logical end must end in the traditions of self-
unfoldment which have developed in the East.

Behind the so-called neurotic trouble, it is
spiritual disquiet, the general dissatisfaction of
man with himself, that is driving him to seek
help from the therapist. In the various forms
of psychotherapy we have consciously and
unconsciously adopted the traditional method
of Yoga—uncovering and disentanglement, which
is slowly making us conscious of our natural
goal and correct identity. Through their continuing quest in this direction, modern psychologists
are bound to recognize that man's true being is
not eog-consciousness, nor his psychological
processes but the calm and tranquility of Being,
awareness, love and bliss.

# Behavior Therapy and Yoga

*by*

John Harvey, Ph.D.

Behavior therapy could be seen as epitomizing the western empirical approach to knowledge. Its roots lie in several assumptions that emerged during the first part of the twentieth century. The first of these was the idea that only that which can be observed, measured and recorded is true. A second assumption stemming from this first was that subjective mental events could not be observed, measured and recorded and were therefore not appropriate subject matter for scientific psychologists. Instead, psychologists should study observable behavior.

The study of observable behavior was originally carried on to a large extent with animals. Rats, pigeons and mice were methodically studied as to how they acquired and lost observable behavior patterns. From these studies arose two basic learning paradigms. The first, known as classical conditioning, is exemplified in the experiements that Pavlov did with dogs. A bell was rung as dogs were fed. Soon the dogs learned to respond to the bell alone with the salivating that normally accompanied presentation of food. In other words, the dogs had been conditioned to respond to the bell.

The second paradigm is known as operant learning. Here the focus is on the consequences that follow a response. If the consequences are reinforcing, the probability of the response's occurring will increase. If the consequences are negative, the probability of the occurrence will decrease. That is, if a rat received a pellet for pushing a bar, it would learn to push the bar more often; conversely, if it received a shock when it pushed the bar, it would learn to push the bar less often.

It was only in the late 1950's that these learning principles came to be applied therapeutically to humans on a large scale. Since then, the applications of behavioral principles have grown exponentially. With this growth the definition of what constitutes behavior has also expanded. Observable behavior has come to include an entire range of physiological responses such as galvanic skin response, brain wave frequencies, and even levels of hormone secretions. Likewise, even the thoughts a person has are considered behavior which is learned and can therefore be changed.

In the formulation of yoga psychology, observation of behavior also played an important role. The yogic *asanas* or physical postures were derived in part from careful observation of various animals. Concerned with the problem of maintaining and improving physical health, the ancient yogis carefully noted what the animals did to keep themselves healthy. They began to imitate animal poses and note the effects. Those poses which had beneficial effects were then incorporated into the system of yogic *asanas*. In this manner such postures as the cobra, locust, lion and pigeon were developed.

The yogis also observed the natural ways in which animals kept themselves clean. Again they imitated, experimented and developed a system of *kriyas* or cleansing exercises. An example of this can be seen in a cleansing process known as the upper wash. It was observed that tigers after digesting a meal would regurgitate the waste products remaining in the stomach. Based on this observation yogis developed the *kanjur kriya* or upper wash, wherein the student swallows a volume of salt water and then regurgitates it.

This practice removes waste from the digestive system.

It can be seen that both yogis and behaviorists studied the behavior of animals and applied their observations to humans. In both cases the emphasis was on testing hypotheses and techniques.

The yogis applied this practical, concrete experimenting to themselves as well. They conducted research on emotions and mental processes. They began with observation of their own behavior and noted the mental and physiological consequences. Working within this tradition of experimenting with themselves, they were able to go deep into this realm. They began to observe the various functions of the mind and developed a classification system for these functions. They noted four aspects of the mind which they labeled *ahamkara* (ego or I sense), *manas* (lower or instinctive mind), *chitta* (mind stuff, or memory bank) and *buddhi* (intellect and will). By carefully watching these different functions within their own minds, they began to understand behavior in terms of the interaction between the different parts of the mind, the senses and the environment. Inner exploration led to the delineation of four states of consciousness known as waking, dreaming, deep sleep

and the superconscious state. The final state
goes beyond the workings of the mind.

## Basic Differences Between Behavioral Approach and Yoga Psychology

The most fundamental difference between the
two approaches resides in their basic veiw of the
world. Learning theory is rooted in the western
empirical approach to the world. Here reality
is essentially that which can be measured and
recorded. This approach has brought tremendous
progress in the physical sciences, where underlying
laws have been discovered that allow for prediction, manipulation and control of the phenomenon
under study.

Behavioral psychology represents an attempt to
make psychology as "scientific" as the physical
sciences. The crucial assumption that is brought
from the physical sciences and applied to the
human psyche is that matter is the essential
building block of the universe. This assumption
is supported by a generally accepted view of
evolution that sees a primordial "soup" of matter
as the basis for all creation. From this "soup"
evolved progressively higher forms of organisms.
Man himself emerged and somehow consciousness
appeared. The inference is that truth can be

known by studying matter and truth about humans can be known by studying behavior, which is matter in measurable action.

The world view of yoga is somewhat different. Here consciousness is seen as the source of ultimate knowledge and truth. From consciousness evolves intelligence, energy and finally matter. Such a non-materialistic approach indicates the need for a different method to study man. In this framework man is seen to consist of five sheaths. The physical or food sheath is the outermost, then the vital or energy sheath, then the mental sheath, the intellectual sheath, and finally the blissful sheath. This means that the study of matter is the grossest plane on which the phenomena of the world can be studied. Appropriate methods must be devised to study these various sheaths of man; techniques used on the material level may not be applicable to the other levels.

This difference in view leads to an appreciation of the difference in the scientific methods of behavioral and yoga psychology. The techniques of behavioral psychology are grounded in the material approach. They emphasize objective mathematical measurement. Proof is always tentative and always based on the amount of measured evidence compiled. In yoga psychology a method has been developed that allows for research into the different levels of man. This method is essentially experiential. Results of each experimenter provide hypotheses for the next. The *Yoga Sutras* of Patanjali are an example. These aphorisms came from an oral tradition based on the experiences of many sages. Essentially they are suggestions as to the results that could occur if the procedures mentioned were applied. The proof in this system is individually experiential. Each person must validate these aphorisms personally. Specific techniques of concentration and meditation are needed to perform this kind of inner research. Concentration trains the mind to be a scientific instrument. Meditation allows for the observation of behaviors of the more inward sheaths described above.

A further contrast between the yogic and behavioral approaches can be seen in the area of goals. In behavior therapy the most important goal is control of behavior. This means either increasing or decreasing the frequency of a particular response. The most important reason for exercising this control is to bring the behavior in line with the expectations and norms of the specific culture. In this light, control, or more specificially self-control, is seen as the ultimate in socialization. The focus of the behavioral approach could be understood as the achievement of harmony with the external environment.

In yoga harmony with the culture and society is seen as a partial goal. In yoga, control over the physiological environment is attained through the practice of asanas, breathing exercises and relaxation techniques. Control over one's social environment comes through study and application of the *yamas*, or behavioral restraints. These restraints are: non-violence (*ahimsa*), non-lying (*satya*), non-stealing (*asteya*), sensual restraint (*brahmacharya*) and non-possessiveness (*aparigraha*). However, asanas and yamas are seen as a preliminary step to internal control. Harmony with the social and physiological environments sets the stage for control of the inner sheaths, i.e., the pranic, mental and intellectual sheaths. The reason for control of the sheaths embraces a humanistic aim long familiar to western thought, the fullest development of the individual's potential, or as it is termed in the East, Self-Realization.

## A Technique of Behavior Therapy: Systematic Desensitization

Although there are considerable differences in the world view, scientific method, and the goals of yoga and behavior therapy, there are some remarkable similarities in the practical applications of these two psychological approaches. The similarities are quite striking in terms of their physiological approaches to therapy.

By the late 1930's western researchers had found that physiological relaxation and psychological anxiety were incompatible states. In other words, if a person were completely physically relaxed, it would be impossible for him to be anxious. Later research on anxiety revealed the complexity of the physiological aspects of the anxiety response. It was discovered that cortical arousal in the case of anxiety led to a wide range of physiological changes mediated by the autonomic nervous system. These changes affected heart rate, blood volume, skin temperature, sweat gland activity, respiration, pupillary change, hormonal changes, gastrointestinal activity, muscle tremors and muscle tension. Moreover, they found that such responses could not only be triggered by external stimuli perceived through the senses, but that symbolic presentations in the form of images, ideas and memories could also initiate an anxiety response.

Joseph Wolpe integrated these facts into a treatment package known as *systematic desensitization.* He considered that anxiety was learned via the classical paradigm. In other words, the person had become conditioned to respond with anxiety to a neutral stimulus. He proposed to break this link by systematically pairing a relaxed physiological state with mental images that progressively approximated the most feared stimulus.

In this approach, the client is taught procedures for relaxation based on the systematic contraction and relaxation of various muscle groups within the body. Each muscle group is tensed for an interval of five to seven seconds, and then relaxed for at least twenty to thirty seconds. The client's attention is directed to the specific sensations of warmth that follow the relaxation of the muscle groups. Movement to another group of muscles is contingent upon an absence of tension in the first group. The muscle groups may be taken in various progressions, e.g., from feet up to head, or from hands to head to feet. The important factor is the systematic nature of the progression.

When the client has progressed to the point where he can achieve a deep and consistent state of relaxation, he and the therapist collaborate on the construction of an anxiety hierarchy. In such a hierarchy, the client visualizes scenes containing the strongest anxiety-eliciting stimulus and moves stepwise down to the weakest. For example, if the anxiety stemmed from public speaking, the most fearful stimulus might be standing on the podium before an audience of 1,000, whereas the weakest stimulus might be holding a copy of a letter inviting the client to speak. Then a series of scenes would be constructed, slowly progressing from the weakest to the strongest stimulus; it might include such events as answering the letter, beginning to write the speech, rehearsing the speech the night before the event, etc.

The actual process of desensitization begins as the client goes into a state of deep relaxation. Then the therapist directs the client to visualize the scenes and maintain the relaxed state. Slowly, under the direction of the therapist, he will move up the hierarchy, progress contingent upon maintaining the state of relaxation. Finally the client will be able to visualize the final scene without any increase in anxiety. Progress in desensitization sessions should ideally accompany real world exposure to these stimuli, successfully visualized without anxiety. Considerable evidence of the efficacy of systematic desensitization has been compiled.

For those familiar with the relaxation techniques of hatha yoga, some of the procedures of desensitization should appear quite similar. In fact, in yoga the key to effective relaxation is this same systematic way of going through the entire body. However, in yoga, relaxation is tied in with many other aspects of self development; thus the essential paradigm of pairing muscular relaxation with anxiety takes on greater breadth and depth.

## Yoga Relaxation

In yoga, relaxation is seen as one of the most important aspects of gaining control over the physical level or sheath. Physical relaxation is important for several reasons. First, it is felt that one must still the body in order to gain access to the mind. When the body is relaxed and quiet one may begin the inner explorations. But there is also an issue of energy ecology involved— unnecessary muscular tension simply wastes energy. Dr. Steven Brena in *Yoga and Medicine* describes the average man as "an absolutely anti-economic machine requiring a great quantity of fuel to supply a very limited work."[1]     In yoga, efficient use and control of energy or *prana* is seen as an important aspect of self-development. In this light, muscular tension is an obstacle to be overcome. Relaxation is seen as a means of bringing balance to the human system. In an ecological sense, needless physiological and emotional arousal is seen to take a toll on the bodily systems, e.g., nerves, glands, and circulation. Proper relaxation helps maintain the health of these systems.

Finally, it is believed in yoga that a relaxed state facilitates a more effective response. Considerable evidence has been compiled in the West to show that over-arousal reduces the effectiveness of performance. One of the goals of yogic relaxation is to prevent over-arousal, to keep the person in a state where responses to stimuli are as effective as possible. A good example is that of the cat, which patiently waits by the mousehole in a completely relaxed but alert state. When the mouse appears the cat will respond, using all its resources. Mastery of relaxation allows one to bring poise into action.

In experimenting with relaxation techniques, the yogis again studied animals, particularly animals in states of relaxation, sleep and hibernation. Two major relaxation poses were developed: in the crocodile pose, the student lays on his stomach, feet apart, arms folded in front, forehead resting on the folded arms; in the corpse pose, the student lies on his back, feet apart, toes pointed outward, arms alongside the body a few inches away, hands resting palms up. The position customarily used for teaching relaxation in systematic desensitization is similar to the corpse pose, but in yoga more attention is given to such details as the position of the hands and feet. The outstretched fingers and open palms form a *mudra* or pose designed to create a psychological state—in this case, a state of acceptance and relaxation.

Contractions and relaxations of muscle groups would, in yoga, be a preliminary to acquaint the student with the various parts of his body and make him aware of his musculature. Actual relaxation begins with what is known in the West as auto-suggestion. The student is taught to systematically travel through each part of the body, asking and suggesting that it relax. This auto-suggestion is used with those parts of the body normally associated with voluntary control.*

Research in biofeedback has shown that bodily functions once thought impossible to control can indeed be controlled. Skin temperature, heartbeat and blood pressure are examples. The adepts in yoga have long insisted that man can gain control over many involuntary functions. This control includes being able to relax these functions.

* The reader should not infer that yoga is basically a process of auto-suggestion. Auto-suggestion is used only in certain preliminary techniques aimed at countering negative suggestions.

This process has been described as one in which the conscious mind sends suggestions to the unconscious mind, which in turn orders the involuntary functions to relax. Thus the adept student can learn to relax internal organs such as the kidneys, liver, stomach, heart, brain, etc.

Deeper stages of relaxation deal more with the mind. Here the breath is mobilized to play an important role. Techniques of even breathing and proper diaphragmatic breathing relax both body and mind. First of all, proper diaphragmatic breathing allows for efficient elimination of wastes and adequate intake of oxygen. Even breathing provides for a balance between fuel intake and waste removal. But beyond this, the breath is seen as a link between body and mind. Slow, rhythmical breathing calms the mind and induces feelings of peace and harmony. Still deeper stages of relaxation are achieved by dis-identifying oneself with the body, mind and ego sense. This is followed by identification with pure consciousness of the universal Self. This final level of relaxation is called spiritual relaxation.

**Yoga and Desensitization**

Yogic relaxation techniques embrace and extend beyond the relaxation techniques in systematic desensitization. What parallels can be found in terms of the actual desensitization to anxiety-producing stimuli? Do yogic practices decondition the student to specific anxiety-arousing stimuli? And finally, do the yoga techniques have benefits extending beyond the desensitization paradigm?

Before answering these questions, the assessment of anxiety responses should be considered. This has been a problem area for behavior therapists. Direct assessment of physiological responses is, for the sake of practicality and expense, largely limited to peripheral measures that record body fluids, electrical activity, sound or volume changes. Such measures are vulnerable to a number of artifacts, especially environmental stimuli. Examples of these artifacts include heat, light, time of day, size of the person, etc. Another approach has involved observation of physiological effects, interference in performance and approach-avoidance behaviors in the presence of a feared stimulus. With observation extreme reactions are easy to spot, but small or subtle differences are difficult to perceive. Another difficulty is the problem with inter-rater reliability or the different way two observers might see and record the same action.

Because of these difficulties considerable use

has been made of self-report forms of assessment. Here the client either describes what he is experiencing or answers test questions designed to discern an anxiety response. In either case, it is important that the client be able to correctly and as objectively as possible view his reactions. The yoga student is trained precisely in these skills of self-observation. While performing asanas, he learns to watch his muscular and skeletal systems. The yogic techniques of relaxation acquaint him with a relaxed state, providing a standard to which various states of arousal can be compared. The practice of meditation trains the student to watch but not get involved in the fluctuations of his mood and the modifications of his mind.

Any deconditioning procedure requires accurate assessment of an anxiety response. The training a yogi receives in self observation would be a great asset to the systematic desensitization process. However actual deconditioning in the yoga framework is considerably more informal than the procedures used in systematic desensitization. Such deconditioning would largely occur during the practice of meditation. As a disturbing or anxious thought arose, the meditator would allow it to pass through his mind. This process might be labeled "letting go." The meditator maintains his relaxed physical and mental state and lets the image go. "Letting go" might be seen as an application of pairing relaxation with an anxiety-producing stimulus. This process is said to de-energize that stimulus and weaken its anxiety-provoking effects.

Learning theorists might label letting go as an ongoing deconditioning or desensitizing process. This is exactly the role that letting go plays in meditation. In yoga psychology it is believed that a continual train of images parades through the mind. Some of these images are pleasing or neutral while others are linked in some degree to fear producing memories. Many of these images are essentially conditioned, anxiety-arousing stimuli. One of the central purposes of meditation is to gradually sever these conditioned links. This is accomplished by pairing the relaxed physical and mental state with the anxiety producing image and letting go.*

Meditation is a continual practice of uncovering these learned fears and anxiety responses. The deeper the student goes into meditation, the more skilled he becomes at uncovering the roots of conditioned anxiety. This in part explains why several studies have shown experienced

---

* The meditator also learns to let go of images to which he is attracted, for these images too lead to arousal and can disturb one's equilibrium.

meditators to have less reported anxiety and psychosomatic illness than novice meditators. These novices in turn show lower levels of anxiety and psychosomatic illness than non-meditators[2]. Thus the letting go and uncovering make meditation an ongoing, generalized desensitization process. These yogic practices do, however, lack specificity. In that instance where a conditioned anxiety was having an extremely disruptive effect on a person's life, the procedures of systematic desensitization would seem to be the most helpful.

## In Vivo Desensitization and "Calm"

There are several new methods of desensitization which show similarities to some of the practices of yoga. The first of these is called *in vivo desensitization*. It is used when the feared stimulus is a concrete physical object or situation. Real stimuli are used rather than imagined or visualized representations of these stimuli. A person afraid of guns might first be told to sketch one, then be given a water pistol, next a small handgun and finally a rifle. Progress through these stimuli would depend upon his maintaining a relaxed state. Often the client may be instructed to gradually approach the actual stimuli outside the therapist's office. He should stop when anxiety increases and continue to approach only when complete relaxation has been re-achieved.

This technique is considered to have the important advantage of being clearly generalizable. It can be applied to real life situations. Any change that occurs is not limited to the therapist's office. Sometimes it is used in conjunction with systematic desensitization to see if the improvements to the visualized hierarchy apply to a real life situation.

A similar technique is differential relaxation. Here the client observes himself in a live situation that may produce anxiety. He analyzes which muscle groups are needed for the activity at hand and selectively relaxes all other muscle groups. In this manner the client can inhibit the general level of arousal and also reduce tension-caused fatigue.

In both of these procedures there are two crucial elements; the first is self-observation and assessment. In *in vivo desensitization*, the person must be able to note slight increases in anxiety and in the accompanying arousal. In differential relaxation, he must have enough awareness of his physical body to accurately note which muscle groups are involved in the performance of the task at hand. The second crucial factor is the ability to relax. This relaxation is either total or selective.

In yoga the student is given extensive training in both of these areas. In the asanas he is taught to observe the action and reactions of his body. In meditation he examines the thoughts flowing through his mind. The yoga student becomes practiced in noting arousal and anxiety. Similarly he has at hand a variety of techniques for achieving relaxation, such as mental relaxation of the body and techniques of even breathing. Thus he would be prepared to apply these two behavioral approaches in the context of therapy.

It is important to note, however, that *in vivo desensitization* and differential relaxation are generalizable to another context. Behavior therapists maintain that they can be applied to new and unanticipated anxiety-causing situations. This means that the person trained in these techniques would have an effective means for dealing with new problems as they arise. He would carry something out of therapy that he could do on his own. Since the yoga student is well trained in self-assessment and relaxation, which are operations of *in vivo desensitization* and differential relaxation, he is particularly well equipped to deal with novel anxiety-provoking objects and situations.

A further behavioral technique that gives promise of being generalizable to a wide range of circumstances is conditioned relaxation. Here the client learns first to achieve a deep state of relaxation, then a voluntary response is made. Typically it is a word like "calm" or "relax." When deeply relaxed, the client is instructed to concentrate on his breath and subvocalize the word "calm" as he exhales. The client practices this until he can achieve relaxation by subvocalizing the word with an exhalation. Then the client is tested. He is presented with an anxiety-producing stimulus and told to subvocalize the cue word together with his exhalation. If he successfully achieves relaxation it is felt he can apply this cue word-exhalation technique to any anxiety producing real life situation.

This technique shows some remarkable similarities to mantra meditation. The mantra in effect is a cue word. The continued practice of mentally repeating the mantra while in a firm but relaxed position builds an association to a centered state. Quite often meditators describe how they "go to their mantra" to calm and center themselves in tense or chaotic situations. But a mantra is more than just a cue word. Not only is it associated with states of relaxation, but is a particular configuration of sound vibrations designed to cause and create a state of calmness and centeredness. The use of mantra meditation is another tool used in yoga psychology along with suggestion, muscle relaxation and regulation of the breath, which lead one to overcome anxieties and fears and maintain a state of alert relaxation through the stresses of day to day living.

## Summary

Psychological approaches which initially seem to be quite disparate often reveal considerable similarity. This seems to be the case with yoga and behavior therapy. At first glance it would seem that the pragmatic behaviorist would have little to do with the mystical yogi. In fact it appears that the approaches to mystical insights consist of many techniques that are extremely practical in terms of dealing with the problems of everyday living. This is one of the reasons that increasing numbers of westerners are taking up the practice of yoga.

At the same time it can be seen that behavioral techniques are moving into surprising areas. Bio-feedback is showing that control over previously presumed involuntary responses can be learned. The field of behavioral self-control points out that people can learn to apply behavior techniques independently. This allows them first to solve their own problems and to chart their own course of development. Finally, the range of behaviors considered changeable has expanded into the area of thoughts. Systems such as rational emotive therapy look at the thought patterns that precede our feelings and actions, and try to teach new thought patterns.

All these advances in the behavioral realm demand considerable skill in self assessment. The techniques of yoga have a number of valuable things to offer in this respect. This suggests an increasing interaction between yoga and behavior therapy. However it must be kept in mind that as of now, yoga and behavior therapy are grounded in radically different views of the nature of truth and reality. This has an important effect on the ultimate goals of each system of psychology. In behaviorism, although the definition of what constitutes a behavior may change considerably, the goals remain framed in terms of the prediction and control of behavior. In yoga, the ultimate goal is the achievement of the highest state of consciousness, the fullest realization of the self.

Bibliography

1 Brena, Steven P., *Yoga and Medicine.* New York: Julian Press, 1972.

2 Goleman, Daniel, "Meditation Helps Break the Stress Cycle," *Psychology Today,* 9, (February, 1976) pp. 82-93.

Paul, Gordon L., and Bornstein, Douglas A., *Anxiety and Clinical Problems: Systematic Desensitization and Related Techniques.* Morristown, New Jersey: General Learning Press, 1973.

Thoreson, Carl E., and Nahoney, Michael J., *Behavioral Self Control.* New York: Holt Reinhart and Winston, 1974.

Ullman, Leonard P., and Krasner, Leonard, *A Psychological Approach to Abnormal Behavior.* Englewood Cliffs, New Jersey: Prentice Hall, 1975.

# Yoga Encounter Groups

*by*

## Phil Nuernberger, Ph.D.

Yoga, far from being some mystical practice for the entertainment of self-proclaimed seekers of truth or religion, is actually an extremely practical psychological system which has the potential of revolutionizing western therapeutic methods. This chapter is about the application of yoga psychology to a therapeutic process, that of encounter groups. Yoga-encounter groups originated three years ago in Minneapolis under the direction of the author. Now yoga-encounter as part of yoga-therapy, is being taught to professionals throughout the country under the auspices of the Himalayan Institute. What are the unique characteristics of yoga-encounter groups? Other than the therapist or group

leader being trained in yoga,* are there any
other characteristics which distinguish yoga-
encounter from other forms of therapy, encounter
or growth groups? I will attempt to answer these
questions.

The psychology of yoga-encounter is unique in
both its philosophy and its techniques, which
have their basis in classical Raja (Astanga) Yoga.
There are four major principles of Raja Yoga
which provide the fundamental framework of
yoga encounter (and therapy). These four
principles are:

1) **Identity**: SELF-awareness, the conscious
   experience of the Superconscious state, or
   Transpersonal Self.


2) **Non-Attachment**: A mode of neutral observation of mental and physical events
   (the Witness).


3) **Karma**: Individual responsibility for one's
   relationship to the world and his/her
   behavior in the world.


4) **Samskara**: Behavior as a mental event.

---

* The importance of the practice of yoga for the therapist is
discussed briefly at the end of this chapter. A more in-depth
discussion by the author is in print for a later publication.

Before discussing these four principles and their relationship to yoga-encounter groups, a word or two about techniques is relevant. Yoga-encounter is eclectic in terms of techniques. Almost any western psychological technique can be used in yoga-encounter. The therapist is free to draw from any training or background experience he or she might have. However, these techniques are used in such a way as to facilitate the development and experience of SELF-awareness as outlined in Raja Yoga. In addition to these, yoga also provides very powerful and exacting meditation, breathing and physical exercises which are designed to facilitate the development of SELF-awareness, calm the mind, and lead to self-mastery.* Later we shall illustrate the use of different techniques as they relate to the fundamental concepts of yoga-encounter.

## Principles

The fundamental assertion of yoga is that one's true identity is a state of Pure Consciousness, called the SELF which can be consciously experienced as the true "I" of the individual.

---

* SELF in caps refers to the Transpersonal SELF; self in lower case letters refers to our ordinary or "normal" experience of personality or sense of I-ness.

Recognition of the Transpersonal SELF, is of profound value in achieving self-mastery which has been largely unobtainable by all the sophisticated techniques of western psychology.

It is a well-known fact that objective observation is the *sine quo non* of scientific study. In Western psychology, mental events are considered to be "subjective" and subject to many perceptual, emotional and cognitive distortions. In particular, when one attempts to analyze his own personality, there is always the distortion created by the Ego's defense mechanisms. Such data obtained through subjective analysis is generally considered to be almost useless as scientific data. In fact, the *only* personal event which seems available for scientific analysis as pure data is behavior. Since it alone is objective, i.e., can be observed by a neutral observer, it is considered to be the only valid data for a scientific psychology. Consequently, western psychology has been developed primarily on the basis of behavior.

It is important to recognize that the designation of mental events as "subjective" is correct in as much as western psychology, philosophy and science believe that *consciousness is a function of, and thus dependent on, the structure called mind.* If this is so, consciousness is limited by this structure and subject to the changes within the structure. Mind is thus the seat of the personality and that which determines existence. Without the mind, there is no existence. This theoretical assumption based on limited experience and logical analysis has been elevated to the realm of dogma.

The assertion that subjective data is open to distortion is undoubtedly correct. Another way of stating this is that when one identifies (in other words, has an emotional attachment) with that which he is studying, the result is a lack of clarity of perception and a distortion of data. The greater the identification, or stronger the emotional attachment, the greater the danger of distortion. Consequently, self-analysis is usually self-deception.

The basic assumption that consciousness is a function of mind allows no way to make that subjective data available for direct objective analysis. We come to the conclusion that the mind cannot directly study its own processes. For this reason, in western psychology subjective realities are interpreted indirectly through study of external behavior. As long as we operate on the assumption that consciousness is dependent on mind, and that mind is the originating cause of awareness, then self-study and introspection will always be subject to distortion. There is no escape from the structure of mind, thus direct objective observation of mental events is impossible.

Furthermore, people tend to confuse the experience of an emotion with objective knowledge of the emotion. While it is the case that one must experience his emotions in order to have objective knowledge of the emotions, it is also the case that experiencing emotions without observing their on-going process only provides an experience, not knowledge of the underlying dynamic structure. The more one is identified with the experience of the emotions, the less he is able to understand the experience and thus the underlying structure. Without neutral direct observation of the inner event and the consequent knowledge of the underlying event, we remain a prisoner of the unconscious dynamics of the event, subject to the conditioning contingencies to which those underlying structures react.

In contrast to western psychology, Yoga therapy begins with the experience and recognition that *mind is an expression of, or vehicle for, Consciousness*. That is, beyond the structure (or process) we call our mind, there is a Superconscious state, the Transpersonal SELF, which is not subject to the forces of the material world.

This is the true identity of man which can be consciously experienced. This SELF is not subject to space/time and thus cause/effect relationships. Therefore, the SELF is not subject to the conditioning process that molds and shapes the mind and personality.

The conscious experience of the Transpersonal SELF, no matter how slight at first, is the basis for a powerful therapeutic tool. The power of this experience lies in the change of identity from a conditioned self, subject to pleasure, pain and change (destruction) to an identity with a SELF that transcends conditioning and change. As the individual increases his ability to experience this Transpersonal SELF, this state of Pure Awareness, he also increases his ability to be uneffected by the flow of mental/emotional events. At the same time he achieves an inner calm and tranquility which allows for a freer and less interrupted flow of mental processes. In other words, *the mind becomes an object of Consciousness (Awareness), available for objective study by the individual*. The awareness and experience of the mind as "not I" allows the mind to be studied like any other object.

Meditation is the primary technique by which one begins to calm the mind, and to direct attention inward where he begins to experience the various levels of Consciousness. This is a gradual process of slowly expanding one's conscious awareness into an awareness of the SELF or Superconscious state and gradually developing the ability to observe the functioning of the mind. This gradual process is the development of *non-attachment.* As the identity of the individual begins to switch from the structure of mind to that of the Transpersonal SELF, he begins to experience mental and behavioral events from an impersonal perspective. He experiences events as happening around him but not to him. As the individual becomes more of the witness, or neutral observer, to on-going events, he simultaneously becomes less emotionally involved with them. Through the process of meditation we achieve the ability to perceive the world in a fashion not tied to the habitual ways of thinking, feeling and acting that have dominated our lives. By developing non-attachment, the individual is able to act directly, simply and effectively in situations where previously he would have reacted from a conditioned response to an emotional involvement.

The remaining two principles of yoga psychology must be mentioned before discussing their practical application in yoga-encounter. *Karma* literally translated means action. Yoga recognizes that each individual is responsible for his mental and physical actions. The law of karma is a recognition of the significance of cause and effect. According to this law, actions create reactions. The individual is constantly shaping his reality by the actions he takes and is responsible for the consequences of his previous actions. In Biblical terms, this is stated: "As ye sow, . so shall ye reap." Responsibility does not mean blame or guilt. Responsibility is the complete acceptance of the consequences of one's actions as well as the fact that one has chosen these actions, be they mental, emotional or behavioral. Taking responsibility in yoga means to increase awareness of the realtionships and consequences of one's thoughts, words and deeds.

The strongest and most subtle karma are mental/emotional actions. In yoga, mental actions, *samskaras*, are seen as the true antecedent causes of behavior. All actions (behaviors) begin and end in the mind. Unless the event occurs in the mind, it cannot occur in behavior. Thus, in order to understand the causes of behavior beyond superficial reinforcement, one must begin to observe and study the antecedent *and* consequent mental actions.

While yoga psychology agrees with western psychology that the personality is a result of conditioning and learning, yoga does not agree that self-mastery or self-control can be achieved through the manipulation of reinforcement contingencies. This is not to say that behavioral therapy is not effective. It certainly is, and conditioning is a very powerful and useful tool. The goal of yoga therapy, however, is to teach the individual how to be free from conditioned responding. As long as the individual is identified with the mind and personality, he is subject to manipulation by such reinforcement contingencies and behavioral therapy is quite effective at this level. But as the individual dis-identifies with the personality and mind, and begins to develop the *witness*, he also begins to transcend conditioned responses, and becomes more of a *will-ing* agent rather than a *reacting* agent. Behavioral therapy is less and less effective and necessary as the individual gains greater self-mastery. Behaviorism as a psychology does not and cannot deal with the SELF which is uneffected by cause/effect relationships. New and different principles are necessary as one expands awareness into more autonomous levels of consciousness.

Yoga psychology teaches self-mastery and control through awareness of antecedents, actions, and consequences. Neutral observation of the mind gradually reveals the evolution and movement of samskaras (mental events) before they have gained the momentum or energy that demands external expression in behavior. If we oversimplify and diagram one event, perhaps it would look like this:

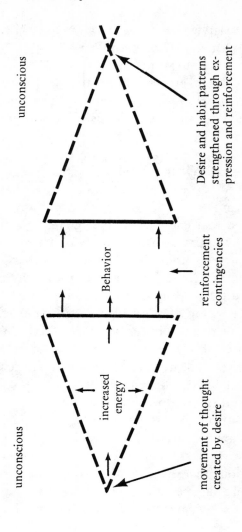

The diagram begins with a mental impression from past experience (samskara). If this samskara is joined with others, momentum accumulates and a desire or want arises to be satisfied. This leads to behavior. The form of the behavior is shaped by the reinforcement contingencies of the pain/pleasure principle.

It is important for our purposes here to recognize that by the time conscious awareness is involved, a tremendous momentum has been built up, and behavior must occur in order to express that energy. An analogy might be helpful here. Picture a man running full-stream down a rather steep hill. Suddenly he sees that just ten feet ahead there is a large drop-off. It is rather difficult to change direction or prevent himself from running off the ledge. You can imagine the difficulty and conflict he would face. But if he had seen the ledge a few feet after he had started down the hill, he could have easily redirected his movement to avoid the ledge while still satisfying his need to run down the hill.

This situation is similar to what happens with our thought patterns. By the time we are normally aware of the particular pattern of thought or emotion, there is little liklihood of control. But as one increases awareness of the samskaras through non-attached observation, the boundary

of the conscious mind is expanded into the unconscious. One learns to control behavior when
one is able to choose which mental impressions to
strengthen through expression and which to gradually eliminate through non-active awareness.
Then behavior modification is in the service of
the SELF, and the individual consciously decides
which thoughts to strengthen and which thoughts
to let weaken and die.

## Yoga Encounter

Yoga-encounter is the application of yoga
psychology combined with western psychology
to teach the individual SELF-awareness in a
group setting. Participants in yoga-encounter
learn skills and techniques which lead to self-
mastery in order that they might develop their
full potential as free, independent human beings.
There are three aspects of the process of yoga-
encounter which are the applications of the
above principles in the development of awareness:
1) Direct conscious experience and knowledge
of the individual's true identity, the Transpersonal SELF.
2) Direct experience and knowledge of the unconscious and the underlying emotional structure which directs and controls the personality.

3) Direct experience of observing mental and behavioral events from the perspective of the witness (developing neutral observation).

The process of yoga-encounter is geared to the development of these three qualities.

Yoga-encounter groups typically consist of 6 to 10 individuals who meet weekly. The group is on-going; new members make an 8 week commitment and are then free to decide how long to continue. Yoga-encounter is a growth-therapy setting where individuals who have a variety of emotional problems to solve, interact with those who have no outstanding emotional problems but are seeking self-knowledge and growth. Psychotic problems are screened out by the therapist and referred to other groups or individual therapy.

The emphasis within the group is on the individual, and not on group processes or communication. The individuals within the group take turns becoming the center of enquiry. This is similar to the "hot seat" of Gestalt groups. While group members are encouraged to work with, or respond to the individual who is "working," the therapist controls the direction of the work and the use of different techniques. The individual is held responsible for his own growth and development.

Since the primary tool for the development and experience of the Transpersonal SELF is meditation, all members of yoga-encounter are required to consistently and daily practice some form of concentrative meditation. Preferably this is yoga meditation using a mantra, but the method used depends on the individual. Basic yoga techniques of relaxation, meditation and breathing are taught to all members. Each group session begins with a relaxation exercise and a short meditation. At times, special meditations are practiced during the group session in order for the group to develop a particular type of awareness. Special concentration and meditation exercises are also taught to individual members when a particular psychological block has been isolated and the individual needs special work to overcome that block.

To better illustrate how yoga-encounter works with the individual, let's follow the case history of one person who participated in a yoga-encounter group. Ron was an intelligent, sincere man involved in upper middle management of a large corporation. In his mid-thirties, he was very successful professionally, but like many professionals, he had begun to wonder about the meaningfulness of his life. His marriage was increasingly rocky as he and his wife realized the lack of communication between them. He had spent about a year reading various books by such authors as Fritz Perls, R. D. Laing and Krishna-murti. Extremely rational, he first presented himself to the yoga-encounter group as someone who really did not have emotions. He could not even understand why people would get enjoyment from a walk into the woods, or along a stream. He was a problem solver, and the best way to solve all problems was with logic.

For Ron, an emotional response was a fearful event, threatening his identity. In order to grow, he needed to accept himself as an emotional being, and to clearly experience these emotions. He also needed to experience how he was selectively using rationality to keep from feeling his emotions. He had to become aware of emotional responses without interfering with the expression of the response, and in such a way that he could clearly understand the controlling unconscious habit structures.

The first step in this process was to supplement his basic yoga meditation with a special focus on the *Anahata Chakra*, or heart center. This heart center is recognized by yoga as the seat of emotional regulation. The yogic experience has been that meditation focused on this heart center develops one's ability to experience and understand his emotions. By directing attention toward this energy center, Ron would slowly expand his capacity to experience emotions. The meditation also served to calm his mind, to begin the process of developing awareness of the Transpersonal SELF and to help him develop the ability to observe mental events from a neutral viewpoint.

To facilitate the development of the Witness, all group members are also taught the art of meditation in action, learning to observe oneself in the midst of activity. In order to do this it is helpful to experience the "inner dialogue" which goes as one is engaged in various activities. Most people are amazed at how much they talk to themselves. What is even more surprising is how dull and pedantic that dialogue is. Ron was no exception. He began to recognize that the constant running stream of conversation he had with himself was the source of considerable tension and apprehension. He also began to be aware of how useful that dialogue was in covering up more subtle mental events. After this recognition, Ron was taught the technique of breath awareness.

By learning to be sensitive to the coolness and warmth of the inhalation and exhalation through the nostrils, and by eliminating the pauses in the breathing process, the individual develops a sense of presence. In other words, he is in greater touch with the *Now* moment. The effect of this breath awareness is to immediately eliminate the inner dialogue. The experience is like taking a wet cloth and wiping the dust off the mind. The individual becomes perceptually aware of the inner and outer environment, free from the systematizing and intellectualizing of an over-cognizing mode of being. He becomes perceptually attuned to on-going events, mental and physical.

Ron (like other group members) was instructed to practice breath awareness while driving, and as often during the day as he could remember. The effect of this practice was to reduce his daily tension levels. He began to be attuned to his feeling states during the day. He was specifically instructed not to analyze these feelings, only to continue to observe them without making any judgments.

During Encounter, Ron was asked to describe what he had learned about himself during the past week. When important feelings were indicated a Gestalt technique was used which led him to experience a rather emotional state. Right before the point of catharsis was reached, the therapist asked him to become aware of his breathing. He was then asked to observe the emotion and not interfere with the body or mind in any way. At this point, the emotional experience was still very intense, and a catharsis was immanent. *By moving into the neutral state of observer (the Witness) through use of yogic breath awareness, Ron was able to allow the experience and catharsis to occur and yet remain observant of the subtle thought and emotional patterns which were immediate and causal to the more consciously powerful but superficial emotional states.*

Ron was able to experience and become aware of those more subtle and usually unconscious causal factors of a rather intense emotional state. He did this by being centered in calmness and tranquillity, while observing without judgment his inner mental/emotional events. Full experience of the emotion was allowed; there was no suppression of the emotional state. But Ron's ability to maintain his identity as the Witness led to the necessary expansion of awareness which allowed him to experience directly and consciously the causal emotional habits rather than merely surface emotions.

This process did not happen once or twice, but several times. At first the individual experiences difficulty observing emotional states. But after practice during group sessions and on his own, he develops the capability of observing intense emotional experiences without the need of the therapist to help him.

Yoga-encounter is *not* interested in teaching individuals to experience emotions for the sake of experiencing emotions. This is only the first step. There is an assumption made by many popular psychologies that sensory and emotional experiencing is the necessary and sufficient basis for enabling the individual to develop his potential. It is assumed that the expression of, and indulgence in, emotions will somehow release all the "negative energies" and leave the individual free from the unhappiness he had previously carried around in the form of suppressed anger, hurt, fear or whatever. Yoga-therapy disagrees with this analysis. In fact, the undisciplined and unobserved expression of emotions only creates new and difficult habit patterns which reinforce the underlying emotional structures.

To feel emotions does not give the necessary awareness to learn control over the emotions. To merely indulge in emotions is rather like allowing the pressure to escape from an overloaded boiler. At times, this may be very necessary, however, when all awareness is focused on the escaping steam, there is no understanding of the steam generating process which forced the expression in the first place. Catharsis is *not* knowledge; it is release. While this release may be necessary, the individual still has not dealt with the causal elements of the catharsis. All attention during a catharsis is usually focused on either the expression itself, or in attending to the external world to gauge the effect of the catharsis on the environment. What doesn't usually happen is a direction of attention inward in order to understand the causal elements that underly the emotional state.

Yoga-encounter is geared toward self-awareness through the observation of the causal dynamic patterns and awareness of the mental and physical consequences of thoughts, emotions and behaviors. By using the cognitive and the emotional faculties, rather than being dominated by either, self-mastery is achieved by awareness and choice, not by will-power and suppression. Only when there is non-attached observation by the Witness is there real progress towards self-mastery and control.

Yoga-encounter recognizes that the individual has absolute power over his relationship to the world. Most people feel out of control of their lives, and in one sense they are. They are not conscious of the choices they are making. From the above description, it is evident that yoga-encounter is an attempt to expand the individual's awareness and allow him to consciously experience his own choices. Language has a very important function in structuring realities. In yoga-encounter, language is used as a tool to facilitate awareness in the individual of the choices he is making. Along with breath awareness, Ron was taught language techniques which he was to practice daily. For instance, he was instructed to choose one word that could be applied to all situations, no matter what they were, or how involved they were. A word such as "interesting" (the author's favorite tool word) or "extraordinary" when applied to all events, mental and physical, leads to the neutral observation of those events. The goal is to break the analytical/judgmental modes of perceptual experience and begin to establish the observational mode. In other words, the goal is to remove the value judgments in order to clearly perceive the consequences of mental and physical events. Ron was eventually able to stop labeling behavior and thoughts. This allowed him to be more receptive to his inner responses. He also found that he was able to remain calm in situations where previously he would have been tense and too caught up in defense mechanisms to clearly perceive what was going on in his mind.

Ron was also instructed to eliminate the phrase "I don't know," and similar phrases when referring to his own emotions or behaviors, and replace those phrases with one like "I do not choose to tell myself." Those familiar with Gestalt psychology recognize that this change in language helps the individual accept the responsibility for his feelings and actions. Likewise, there are no "things" inside one's head. Phrases such as "something made me do it" or "something inside my head" were immediately changed to "I chose to do it" or "I chose not to be aware." In other words, Ron had to become totally responsible for his thoughts and feelings. Saying that "she made me angry" was quickly interrupted during group, and Ron had to restate the sentence in such a way as to accept the responsibility for the anger, e.g., "I chose to be angry." Whether he was conscious of why he chose the anger or not was not the issue. Most of us are not really aware why we choose the emotional responses that we use. The purpose was to force Ron to realize that he did *choose* the response, and that he had the freedom to choose differently. The individual begins to experience that the choice is his, he doesn't have to *react*!

Of course, other individuals bring different problems to encounter group, but all of them

suffer from lack of awareness in one way or
another. There are a great number of meditation
techniques which can be used, depending on the
nature of the individual's pattern of non-
awareness. For instance, there are meditational
techniques which develop one's creative abilities,
or one's ability to surrender to internal guidance,
Other meditational techniques help one to allevi-
ate guilt, to counteract depression, or to eliminate
free-floating anxiety. Some meditation techniques are practiced in a group, some are done by
the therapist and the patient meditating together,
and many are special techniques which may
involve several months of practice by the individual. There are also a wide variety of breathing
exercises which facilitate control of the breath
and in turn develop control over the emotions by
regulating the parasympathetic nervous system.
Hatha Yoga (physical yoga) exercises are also
taught to group members. These not only remove
blocks in body energy, but strengthen the nervous
system and facilitate the development of a calm
and tranquil mind.

As we mentioned early in the chapter, yoga-
encounter is quite eclectic in terms of techniques.
The western world is very sophisticated in psychological systems which provide excellent techniques for developing one's ability to experience

emotions and to manipulate behavior. The successful use of a wide variety of systems only reflects the tremendous variety of individuals and their unique patterns of non-awareness. However, there is no unifying philosophy or systematic approach to the development of full human potential in this hodge-podge of techniques and systems.

Yoga-encounter provides a unifying system by which these diverse approaches can be understood within a coherent framework, that of complete SELF-awareness and self-mastery. In yoga-encounter, all techniques, whether they are yoga exercises, Gestalt, psychosynthesis, behavior modification, or whatever, are directed toward awareness of the subtle unconscious habit patterns which control our lives. The purpose is to expand the conscious part of the mind into the unconscious, slowly and gently, in order to fully comprehend and utilize our full mind.

Notice that throughout the chapter, the emphasis has been on *awareness* and not *change*. Often change is made in ignorance of the underlying dynamics of the behavior. The urge to change is generally an attempt to avoid pain. People want to change because they hurt, they feel some lack (often not definite) of meaning in their lives. The desire for change is all well and good, but often change means only a change in surface structures, and no real awareness of the unconscious motivations. Sometimes the changes work, and sometimes they don't. Often people settle for whatever will dull the pain rather than utilizing that pain to increase awareness.

Yoga-encounter focuses on awareness. SELF-awareness leads to a natural transformation rather than a forced change (forced by pain). Individuals are at different levels in their own development of awareness. Yoga-encounter recognizes that the individual is in the perfect place in order to take the next step into SELF-awareness. In yoga-encounter, there is a recognition that true awareness will lead to natural change, that transformation is the inevitable result of awareness. Transformation can be defined as that change which flows from a calm and tranquil center of identity with the Superconscious State (Trans-personal SELF). Consequently, all techniques are used as a tool for the development of the Witness, and for the use of the Witness, and in this way, all techniques can serve as a springboard for neutral (objective) observation of the mind.

One other facet needs at least to be mentioned. The tremendous potential of yoga-therapy is perhaps for the therapist since yoga frees the therapist from his own personality. Psychologists typically want to spend time studying others;

their behavior, their test results, their interaction with the environment. Yoga teaches you that in order to understand the other person, you must first understand yourself. When the therapist is aware of his own inner dimensions and filtering systems, then he/she will be able to understand others more completely. Self-knowledge means other knowledge. When the therapist is grounded in his Witness, he is able to use his entire mind and body as a receiving station for these signals transmitted by the other person. It is a fallacy to think that we can hide ourselves from others. We are constantly broadcasting all of our secrets, all our personality quirks, our total being. The only reason we don't understand another person is that we are not tuned into and fully aware of our own tremendous perceptual systems, physical and mental and spiritual. When the therapist experiences SELF-awareness, he is able to guide others to the same extent. If you want to teach inner calm and tranquility, if you want to teach inner strength and knowledge, then you must have first-hand experience of these qualities.

The essence of yoga is SELF-knowledge, self-mastery and the development of the full potential of the human being. Yoga-encounter is one path with which to facilitate that development. We share in the Universal Being. It is time we utilize that sharing to develop our potential to its fullest degree.

# About the Writers

**Rudolph M. Ballentine Jr., M.D.** was born in 1941 in Columbia, South Carolina. A physician and psychiatrist, he studied psychology in the United States and France before receiving his M.D. degree from Duke University. He completed a residency and was Professor of Psychiatry at Louisiana State University. He then travelled widely in India learning the deeper aspects of Yoga and studying Ayurvedic Medicine and Homeopathy. He knows several languages including Hindi. A private practitioner of General and Psychosomatic Medicine, he is the Director of the Biofeedback-Meditation and Combined Therapy Programs of the Himalayan Institute's Headquarters. Dr. Ballentine lectures extensively around the country and is the author of *Diet and Nutrition* and *Science of Breath* and co-author of *Yoga and Psychotherapy.*

**Arwind U. Vasavada, Ph.D.** , a Jungian analyst and author, was born in 1912 in Rajasthan, India. He studied at Bombay University, Benares Hindu University and the C. G. Jung Institute in Zurich, Switzerland. Dr. Vasavada has been a university professor in the field of psychology since 1945. He came to the United States in 1970 when he began teaching at the Y.M.C.A. Community College and Roosevelt University, both in Chicago.

**John Harvey, Ph.D.** has a degree in Behavioral Disabilities from the University of Wisconsin and has extensive training in yoga and meditation. He currently works in clinical service, research and training at the Meyer Children's Rehabilitation Institute at the University of Nebraska Medical Center in Omaha, and acts as coordinator of the Counselor's Training Program at the Himalayan Institute.

**Phil Nuernberger, Ph.D.** has a degree in counseling from the University of Minnesota. He has extensive experience in the areas of yoga encounter groups and yoga counseling. He presently conducts seminars in the Stress Management and Research Program of the Himalayan Institute, and is a consultant in the Meditation Center in Minneapolis. He is co-author of *Theory and Practice of Meditation*.

**Swami Ajaya**—Alan Weinstock, Ph.D.—is a practicing clinical psychologist and consultant to several mental health centers. He is the director of the Yoga Meditation Society of Madison, Wisconsin. Swami Ajaya has authored *Yoga Psychology*, co-authored *Yoga and Psychotherapy* and *Emotion to Enlightenment* and has edited *Living with the Himalayan Masters, Spiritual Experiences of Swami Rama*.

# HIMALAYAN INSTITUTE PUBLICATIONS

| | |
|---|---|
| Living with the Himalayan Masters | Swami Rama |
| Yoga and Psychotherapy | Swami Rama, Swami Ajaya R. Ballentine, M.D. |
| Emotion to Enlightenment | Swami Rama, Swami Ajaya |
| A Practical Guide to Holistic Health | Swami Rama |
| Freedom from the Bondage of Karma | Swami Rama |
| Book of Wisdom | Swami Rama |
| Lectures on Yoga | Swami Rama |
| Life Here and Hereafter | Swami Rama |
| Marriage, Parenthood & Enlightenment | Swami Rama |
| Meditation in Christianity | Swami Rama, et al. |
| Superconscious Meditation | Usharbudh Arya, Ph.D. |
| Philosophy of Hatha Yoga | Usharbudh Arya, Ph.D. |
| Yoga Psychology | Swami Ajaya |
| Psychology East and West | Swami Ajaya (ed) |
| Foundations, Eastern & Western Psychology | Swami Ajaya (ed) |
| Meditational Therapy | Swami Ajaya (ed) |
| Diet and Nutrition | Rudolph Ballentine, M.D. |
| Theory & Practice of Meditation | Rudolph Ballentine, M.D. (ed) |
| Science of Breath | Rudolph Ballentine, M.D. (ed) |
| Joints and Glands Exercises | Rudolph Ballentine, M.D. (ed) |
| Yoga and Christianity | Justin O'Brien, Ph.D. |
| Inner Paths | Justin O'Brien, Ph.D. (ed) |
| Faces of Meditation | S. N. Agnihotri, Justin O'Brien (ed) |
| Sanskrit Without Tears | S. N. Agnihotri, Ph.D. |
| Art and Science of Meditation | L. K. Misra, Ph.D. (ed) |
| Swami Rama of the Himalayas | L. K. Misra, Ph.D. (ed) |
| Science Studies Yoga | James Funderburk, Ph.D. |
| Homeopathic Remedies | Drs. Anderson, Buegel, Chernin |
| Hatha Yoga Manual I | Samskrti and Veda |
| Hatha Yoga Manual II | Samskrti and Judith Franks |
| Philosophy of Death & Dying | M. V. Kamath |
| The Practical Vedanta of Swami Rama Tirtha | Brandt Dayton (ed) |
| The Swami and Sam | Brandt Dayton |
| Chants from Eternity | Institute Staff |
| Thought for the Day | Institute Staff |
| Spiritual Diary | Institute Staff |
| Himalayan Mountain Cookery | Martha Ballentine |
| The Yoga Way Cookbook | Institute Staff |